BUBBLY ON YOUR BUDGET

Also by Marjorie Hillis

Live Alone and Like It

BUBBLY ON YOUR BUDGET

LIVE LUXURIOUSLY WITH WHAT YOU HAVE

MARJORIE HILLIS

Drawings by Winifred Murray

CHRONICLE BOOKS

SAN FRANCISCO

FIRST CHRONICLE BOOKS LLC EDITION PUBLISHED IN 2011.
FIRST PUBLISHED IN THE UNITED STATES OF AMERICA IN 1937
by The Bobbs-Merrill Company.

Published in Great Britain in 2009 by Virago Press.
Reprinted in 2010.

Library of Congress Cataloging-in-Publication Data
Roulston, Marjorie Hillis
[Orchids on your budget]
Bubbly on your budget : live luxuriously with what you have / Marjorie
Hillis ; drawings by Winifred Murray.
p. cm.
Originally published in 1937 as: Orchids on your budget.
ISBN 978-1-4521-0235-1 (pbk.)
1. Finance, Personal. 2. Budgets, Personal. I. Title.
HG179.R692 2011
332.024–dc22
2010046401

Ping-Pong is a registered trademark of Parker Brothers, Inc, Corp.
Tintex is a registered trademark of Kiwi Brands, Inc, Corp.

Manufactured in China
Designed by SARAH PULVER

1 3 5 7 9 10 8 6 4 2

CHRONICLE BOOKS
680 SECOND STREET
SAN FRANCISCO, CALIFORNIA 94107

www.chroniclebooks.com

CONTENTS

CHAPTER ONE

WELL,
WHO ISN'T POOR?

AN ASTONISHING number of the people you know, probably including yourself, insist that they have to do a lot of economizing. They not only believe this is true, they *know* it is, and what's more, they're positive they have to do more economizing than the next person. This isn't because of the size of their incomes, or the lack of size; it's because they haven't as much money as they wish they had, which would be true no matter what their income. They have a dream of the way they'd like to live, but it's always just ahead of them, and by the time they've covered the distance, it's moved a little farther on. Their ships are eternally on the horizon and never come in.

Moreover, melancholy though we sound, this seems to be a perpetual state of affairs, having nothing to do with conditions, the Administration (whether you love it or hate it), the price of free gold, or the chance of Inflation. It's just one of the Facts of Life that go on being true, good times or bad. Depression or Boom, six maids and a butler or no maid at all, practically everybody has less money than he or she used to have, or has acquired more expensive tastes. Either thing makes you feel like the well-known mouse with religious affiliations.

As a matter of fact, most of the people who think they're poor are right. For the feeling of poverty isn't a matter of how little money you have—it's a matter of being behind with your bills at the end of the month or not making your income stretch over the things you want. That covers just about all of us except Mr. Ford and Mr. Mellon and a few other plutocrats who don't have to count the cost. We really mean a few, and even they had better not be too sure of week after next. (If there ever was such a thing as security—which the shirtsleeve-to-shirtsleeve tradition makes us doubt—it is now a charming phantom of the past.) All of the rest of us have to budget, or should, and the sensation of having to do so is pretty much the same, whether it means giving up the third limousine or giving up the butter with your meals. (When it comes to giving up the meals themselves, it's destitution, not economy, and it's not the subject of this book, though we reserve the right to touch on it now and then.)

This being the case, we can think of few things more futile than stewing because one hasn't enough money—or few things about which people do more stewing. Enough money for what? Ten chances to one, for a house like the Smiths' or a trip to the Mediterranean or a new evening wrap. We'd like them too, but we don't have to have them, and we'd feel no better in the larger house; the European trip would only start us planning a trip to China; and the solid ermine wrap wouldn't make a hit unless we made one too. What most people don't concede is that, with a little planning and a dash of ingenuity, they might have what they want. They hate to plan (planning about possibilities and daydreaming about improbabilities are not the same things), they detest the Problem anyway, and they don't want to make the effort needed to Do Anything About It. They want bubbly on their budgets—but that's as far as they get.

This isn't very intelligent, because almost anyone with spirit can wangle a bottle of bubbly or two, and have a lot of fun besides. We are all for fun *and* bubbly, and we propose to go into the matter in our modest fashion. And we'd like to begin by protesting at the spiritless way in which so many people accept what they refer to as their "lot in life." Granting that each of us has a lot, it doesn't have to be a five-by-seven, or a site on an alley with a wall for a view. This is a universe where, if only you're sufficiently determined to wriggle toward the best, the chances are all in favor of your getting the best, bubbly included. And, as it happens, conditions have never been so favorable for those of us who are not millionaires but still want the bubbly (or orchids, or parties, or attractive apartments).

One helpful fact is that we no longer have to be Substantial. Not so long ago, it was a distinct advantage to be pointed out as a person whose family had been Pillars of Society for a couple of generations, with an impressive bank account and all the paraphernalia that went with it. Unfortunately, you were expected to repeat the performance. Nowadays, this point of view is becoming a little stodgy. Most of the people who Get Around and have the best time seem to come out of the Everywhere into the Here with very little in their pocketbooks. They keep just a couple of laps ahead of their bills, and that only with effort. But what matters is not the margin, or the background; it's the wit that they show in keeping ahead and the grace they display against *any* background.

There are, of course, as many ways of meeting these problems as there are people in the world, but in this matter, they can be divided into two groups. One group includes the people who use their difficulties as an excuse for Letting Things Go, and the other takes in those individuals who have the brains and energy to Do Something About It.

Every circle has its Escapists, of course, who go over the side on the slightest excuse, and especially if their trouble is financial. The most fashionable trick is to Get Away From It All by heading for an island in the South Seas or a cabin in the woods. This is all very well if you have no responsibilities to keep you home and like living on bananas or bear meat. But most of us have to pull up stakes and put them down again a couple of miles from where we started, and we're not too well fitted for the Great Outdoors Life anyway. The people with spirit make the less dramatic change enthusiastically, and those who have ingenuity besides do it smartly.

The most completely spiritless are those who do it with embarrassment, apparently not having observed that being ashamed of a lack of wealth is as dated as a hobble skirt. Lots of the Best People now live in made-over garages, or penthouses that are only slightly transformed attics, and Thrift, in its best forms, is every bit as smart as the advertisements claim.

The one thing you ought to be ashamed of is economizing grubbily. Nobody who matters cares a *pouf* what your income is these days, but people do care how you live and how you act about it. The scale isn't important, but the effect is. There are few things more boring than to see people counting their pennies mournfully or making you uncomfortably conscious of the need for constant counting, and few things more attractive than to see people living charmingly and cheaply. Women who talk poverty and complain about the things they can't have are invariably tiresome, and women who make something gay out of next to nothing are sure to be exciting.

Even quite dull people can live smartly if they have plenty of money, and the money often makes them duller. A slight financial pressure sharpens the wits, though it needn't sharpen the disposition. But it takes an interesting person to have an attractive ménage on a shoestring and to run it with gaiety and charm.

The trick is to have the right attitude, as it is with most things in life. To economize, if you have to economize, with gaiety and an air. It's amazing, considering how

general the problem is, how few people
do this. Anybody can economize drably
and untidily, and a disheartening number do. Most people run down instead of
cutting down. But not the interesting
people. They grasp the somewhat obvious fact that any
problem so pressing is worth conquering, and with as
much zest as possible.

We are not putting forth the Pollyanna-like theory that
you can have just as much fun with very little money as
you can with a lot of it—though everybody knows plenty
of poor people who are happier than the rich ones, to
back up even this unpalatable notion. We are claiming
that, given the right point of view, you can have *enough*
fun, and it doesn't have to be dowdy fun or dimmed
by a forced making-the-best-of-it attitude, which spoils
anything. And we claim that if you sit down and are miserable because you can't have caviar and mink, or even
chicken and caracal, you haven't very much spunk.

We even claim, much as we hate to sound smug, that
most of us could have just as much fun as we're having
now on a lot less money. Worse than that, that we'd have
fun planning how to do it. This isn't as gloomy an idea
as it sounds, and anyway a good many of us will *have* to

have fun on less money. Money is something that changes hands as rapidly as a basketball during a fast game.

If you take out your address book and read through from A to Z, you'll be startled to find that a fair proportion of the people listed have changed their scale of living during the last few years, some of them moving up and more of them moving down. It isn't improbable that if you haven't done the same thing, you may next year. But if you have to, it needn't be a change for the worse, whichever way you go; it can be merely a change to something different. And most of us need a change every now and then.

The first thing *not* to do is to go around complaining about your lot in life. There is no one in the world who can't think up enough causes for complaint to make him (or her) pretty eloquent on this subject, if he really tries, as so many do. There is, for instance, that large group of youngish married women whose children are just old enough not to occupy all their time and whose husbands' incomes are not quite as large as that of the man in the big house on the corner, and who tell you bitterly and repeatedly of the cross they have to bear in not being free to go out in the world and get a job. These ladies see themselves as poor creatures with suppressed genius, or at least talent, beating their wings against a cage. It doesn't occur to them that they have a job that could fill all their time if they did it as well as it could be done, and that their attitude toward it would cause them to be fired (deservedly) in any other. They substitute Well Enough for Superlatively and have a dozen excuses for every weak spot in their performance, and they would be distinctly annoyed if you told them that it was their own fault that they don't find their job more interesting.

There are also the women who go to offices in a martyr-like frame of mind, cherishing the belief that they would be knockouts in the role of devoted wives and loving mothers. Perhaps they would, and then again, perhaps they wouldn't. If you're martyr-like in one role, you're pretty apt to be martyr-like in another. Theories about maladjustment are all very well, but it usually takes only an average amount of intelligence to do a little readjusting if the need is acute.

Whatever your lot in life, it's merely a challenge to your resourcefulness, a set of materials with which to work. Maybe you would rather play polo than Ping-Pong, but if you've got an old Ping-Pong set and no ponies, you'll get a lot more fun out of life from being a Ping-Pong champion than from taking a dispirited whack with a polo mallet every now and then.

CASES

Case I: Mrs. A.—Mrs. A. is a handsome woman with exceptional charm and a great deal of pride. Until recently, she had a dashing husband who belonged to the promoter type and who, when he was rich, was very, very rich and when he was poor was broke. Mrs. A. was visible only during the affluent periods. At these times, the A.'s lived in great elegance on Park Avenue, and Mrs. A. wore clothes from Bendel and entertained in lavish style. Between these periods, they disappeared into oblivion.

Only a few friends ever succeeded in tracking them down during their meager moments and then it was only to find themselves unwelcome in a shabby, badly run house in a cheap suburb. Their hostess was no longer a handsome person; she was merely a large, slovenly woman who had let herself go. She was, moreover, sulky. She showed resentment toward her husband for getting her where she was, resentment toward her guests for finding her there, and resentment toward Life for picking her as the victim of these particular circumstances. The guests, who had genuinely enjoyed Mrs. A.'s wit and good game of bridge even more than her hospitality, and were ready to enjoy them rich or poor, retired in confusion, with that flat feeling that does nothing to help the donor's popularity.

When the A.'s emerged, however, all was more or less as before until the last time.

Recently, Mr. A. had an unusually long period of prosperity, but Mrs. A. did not benefit by it, as he has transferred his affections and his name to a young lady who used to work in a shop and always managed to be chic, well groomed, and cheerful on a very small salary. Personally, we don't consider Mr. A. a great loss, but unfortunately the ex-Mrs. A. (who now seems to have retired into permanent oblivion) doesn't agree with us.

Case II: Mrs. L.—Mrs. L. is married to an artist who has a charming disposition and some talent, but who is an almost total loss at bringing home the bacon. Mrs. L., however, is a wise lady who reasons that if that is the way Mr. L. is made, there is not much that she can do about it except cut the bacon as thin as possible and serve it up with gaiety.

In their two-room-and-kitchenette apartment, she has substituted atmosphere for expensive furnishings, working quite logically on the theory that most of her friends won't know economy from Art. She also makes her own appearance contribute to the decoration, occasionally using the same principle quite shamelessly and very successfully. She does all the work, including the family laundry, but she keeps a mirror over the kitchen sink, exercises to keep her figure trim and flat, and always has one dress on hand that makes her look more like a countess than most real ones do. When she can't manage a dress in the current style, she maneuvers an old one into a period effect and wears it without apology, often causing envy in her friends' bosoms.

In addition, she goes to all the free exhibits, knows a hundred fascinating facts about the museums in her city, makes the most of the nearest public library, and reads all dramatic criticisms in the paper so consistently that you'd never guess she hadn't been to all the best plays.

When you drop in to see her, Mrs. L. serves you tea and paper-thin slices of bread and butter with such an air that you think she's chosen these refreshments from among a hundred tea-time possibilities; and you probably berate your own maid later for the vulgar profusion of food that usually accompanies your tea. Mrs. L. also discusses current goings-on with such a fund of information and animation that you wish you could get around as she does.

Mrs. L. agrees with the ladies who envy her her lot, since they, she realizes, are not married to Mr. L.

(We are glad to report that Mr. L. appreciates her.)

Case III: Miss S.—Miss S. is an almost penniless young woman who feels that the world owes her a living and is pretty remiss about paying up. She is firmly determined to get what she thinks she deserves out of life, but she has no intention of working for it. Her method, therefore, is to use all her wiles and ingenuity in wangling invitations (preferably for weekends or longer) out of her friends and stretching the duration of her visits as much as possible. Between times, she parks with her relatives.

Miss S. is not unattractive and she swims, dances, and flirts with at least average expertness. She is also almost always available to hostesses needing an Extra Woman—a fact that makes her rating fairly high on guest lists.

She is, of course, denied the privilege of choosing where she will go or when, she has to turn on all the charm she has a good share of the time in the houses she visits, and she is not always welcome in her relatives' establishments. But she has not yet realized that she works harder and for longer hours than most girls with nine-to-five jobs, and that while they are building up reputations for efficiency that will be profitable in the future, the only reputation she is getting is the undesirable one of being a sponger.

CHAPTER TWO

NOT THE OLD HOMESTEAD

WITH MOST of us, home is where the bills are, and a lot of the bills are for the home. This being the case, we are all for starting economy (if there must be economy) in the roof over your head. We know plenty of people who will fight this idea to the death, either from sentiment about giving up the Old Homestead or from a notion that they are Keeping Up Appearances by not moving from where they have always lived. This notion may show a fine proud spirit, but it is definitely antiquated, and the appearances it keeps up are sometimes pretty odd besides. As for the sentiment, we are against it in spite of having a heart as soft as mush.

Today, the impoverished gentlewoman is a dodo. Secret skimping is out, like false bosoms. Those genteel and romantic characters about whom authors love to write, who live in the old family home, chiefly on yams and cornmeal, while it disintegrates around their aristocratic ears, are all very well in literature, but the best you can say for them in real life is that they are quaint. Most modern individuals would rather be crippled than quaint, and quite rightly. Quaintness is stuffy.

It should take less than average intelligence to see that the cost of the place you live in should be only a reasonable proportion of what you have to spend. The fact that things are looking up doesn't alter this principle—it emphasizes it.

More cheer is usually synonymous with more expense outside your household bills. Which means that, if you find that home is eating up your income, the thing to do is to move, no matter how many generations bearing your name have died in the front bedroom. We admit that moving often presents complications, but almost always it can be accomplished if the struggle is sufficiently determined.

The transfer may hurt your feelings, but it shouldn't hurt your pride. Similar moves have been made by Russian royalty, French counts, Spanish nobility, American bankers, an English King, and most of your acquaintances, and if anyone has thought less of any of them, it was not because they moved. Some of the most drastic changes we know of have caused admiration and envy in the breasts of onlookers.

There is, of course, the question of where to move to, and the answers fall into two groups. The first is to find a place equal in size to the one that is getting your bank account down, but of less elegant style and in a cheaper neighborhood. The second is to find an equally good address and go in for condensation. Some emergencies make it necessary to join both schools simultaneously, but even then, all is not lost. (Or if it is, you are in the destitute group already referred to and out of this book— temporarily, we hope.)

Which group you should join depends on the kind of person you are and the kind of family you have, if any— which you should know, but we don't. If you lean to the casual side and are gay rather than grand and more merry than meticulous, you'd better look for the big place and spread out. But if you like everything kept up, to the last leaf on the well-washed ivy, you'll probably be happier in even a very small place on your accustomed rung of the social ladder.

The important thing to do before you even start to look for your new residence is to decide what are the requirements, according to your own special tastes and temperament. Don't just follow the usual rules. There is no place like home for making you either happy or miserable, and which it does is more or less up to you. We know of one woman whose list read: A View, Sunshine, Chic, Gaiety. It looked a little silly, she thought, but it covered the essentials—for her. The point was that all four things were essential, and she kept right on looking till she found a sunny New York apartment within her price, with one end of its small living room given entirely to windows looking over the East River and with an arrangement of its two-and-a-half rooms that could be made extra gay and chic with the help of lots of mirrors and a little paint.

Another young woman headed her list with "A Place for Parties"—which stopped her dead for a time, since her income just about permitted a one-room apartment in her home town of Baltimore. Eventually, however, she found a log cabin in the country on the bank of a decorative stream, and rented it for so few dollars that you wouldn't believe us if we told you. She furnished it with taste and secondhand antiques, of the cottage variety that doesn't cost much, and she now entertains all her friends for gay weekend parties, weather permitting.

These two ladies are mentioned merely to point out that your requirements can be the ones that give you the most fun, regardless of conventionalities. If you'd rather have a fireplace than an up-to-date bathroom, don't let anyone talk you out of it. If you'd get more out of a terrace, however infinitesimal, than either, keep on hunting till you find one. There must be one somewhere, within your price.

Having found what you're looking for, or something that approximates it, the next rule is *not* to move all of the contents of the old four-story house or nine-room apartment into the new two rooms and bath. Pick out the things that you absolutely need and think the rooms will accommodate without crowding and then deduct about a third of those. This may be what you would plan to do anyway, but just wait till the actual moment for doing it comes. It is a curious fact that personal possessions take on fictitious values and exceptional charms when the owner, no matter how generous, is faced with giving them away or even selling them (which usually amounts to the same thing). You may decide that you can get along without the second kitchen table and the rocking chair in the third-story back bedroom, and even throw in the umbrella stand and a couple of Victorian vases, but that is about as far as most people can go without a struggle—which accounts for a lot of clutter, dowdiness, and unnecessary work for the housewife. Yet the truth is—much as we hate to be rude—that it is highly probable that not all of your possessions are museum pieces or even irreplaceable heirlooms, and that some of them are out of date, if not actually ugly. Take the guest room armoire as an example—are you sure that it really is so handsome and that the money you would spend storing it wouldn't buy a better and smarter one by the time you can afford a guest room? As for the pictures you have regarded so tenderly ever since you decided to move—ten chances to one, the house you are in now would have looked a lot better if you had given most of them to the Thrift Shop and had the rest reframed.

If you can bring yourself to the point of throwing out everything that you can't use to advantage in your new establishment, you will be that much better off—but this is unlikely. Our heartless advice, therefore, is to throw out as much as you can bear to without actual pain, and when parting becomes too poignant, to park the rest in some relative's attic or garage. You might drop in to see these prized possessions a couple of years from now, and if—as you look them over without their old, familiar surroundings, or the enhancement added by your own imagination— you don't wonder how on earth you ever lived with them as long as you did, we'll let you give one to us as a present.

The current feeling in decoration is something for you to make the most of, if you've set out to economize. One of its strong points is elimination, which is right up your alley. By going in for it, you can save both in purchasing and in upkeep, to say nothing of saving time and trouble. This is not to say that you should give everything away regardless. You will need some things, we hope, and a reasonable amount of sentiment can enter into your choice without disaster. A lovely old mahogany chest may be the keynote of a room and look as right in a small space as a large one. You will always have a use for fine china and silver and linen, and small tables and lamps can move around like traveling salesmen and still look at home. Our plea is for enough elimination so that your new rooms won't look crowded and so that guests can navigate in comfort.

The point is to do your planning intelligently and enthusiastically. Particularly, enthusiastically. Enthusiasm is the most important ingredient in the furnishing and decoration of any house or apartment, big or little. It, or the lack of it, stands out far more conspicuously than the curtains or overstuffed chairs, giving away your spirit about the whole matter—which is, after all, the thing that counts.

Next in importance comes personality, which has even less than enthusiasm to do with expense. We know of one woman who has an entrancing house in the country, furnished largely with some things inherited from her mother, some office pieces cast off at the time of moving, and some pieces bought here and there in secondhand stores. She didn't fuss about the fact that, having put her ALL into just the house she wanted, she had to use what she had, because she was intelligent enough to realize that, after all, that's what most people have to do. She merely combined styles in her own individual way, regardless of rules, but by no means regardless of effect. All of the walls are white—partly because she's a businesswoman who didn't have time to worry about colors, but more because a fresh, clean, scrubbed look suits her. She emphasized this look in her own bedroom, knowing that she couldn't bear a lace-and-satin effect

and that it wouldn't go with her type anyway. But she put a little drama into the dining room, that being a place where her friends occasionally gather in their best clothes. The decorations, linen, and china aren't extravagant, but they have what she calls *Whoops*. She had as much fun out of the economizing as out of the spending.

Actually, it's not difficult to have fun out of economizing (up to a point), both because of the sense of accomplishment it gives you and because everybody else is doing it too. Today, in the smartest houses, you are apt to find discount store glass mixed with Crown Derby China and the hostess boasting about it. Ladies of unlimited means have themselves a time in bargain basements and secondhand shops, and tell about it to anyone who will listen. They tell, because that kind of shopping takes wit instead of money, and wit is a far less common commodity.

Anybody who can pay for authoritative advice can buy good taste, which is always for sale to those who really want it. But it takes knowledge and, generally, some serious study to show the same level of taste without paying for it. Many people with money don't bother with the authoritative advice, which is why you can usually guess so much about people after a few hours in their houses. The difference between an aristocrat and a member of the bourgeoisie is as plain in her choice of paper napkins as in her selection of embroidered linen.

Your economy may not be a game of wits, but however deadly in earnest it is, it still needn't be drab. If you keep your standards up, even though your salary goes down, it can have an air, which will be all the more impressive because of the courage behind it. You can also have gaiety and charm and chic, if you are ready to substitute the trouble they take for the cash they cost.

Or you can just settle down and let things go to pieces around you. You'll have lots of company.

CASES

Case IV: Mrs. H.—Mrs. H. is a spirited lady whose husband left her a large, impressive house and little else.

The upkeep proved to be beyond her means, but Mrs. H., having energy and imagination, was not fazed by so trivial a fact. Dipping into her meager capital, she proceeded to remodel the brownstone mansion, turning the third and fourth floors into apartments that she rented with the air of a grande dame conferring a favor, and also with profit. The lower floors, which she occupies herself with no loss of pleasure or prestige, have lost none of their former elegance, but have gained in charm under Mrs.

H.'s modern taste and skill. Having spent all she could afford on the two upper stories, her decoration below was accomplished chiefly by taking down two-thirds of the pictures, removing one-third of the furniture, and putting half the knick-knacks on closet shelves. New ivy-patterned curtains and a profusion of huckleberry leaves in white vases accomplished the rest, and a lot of Mrs. H.'s friends are wondering where she got all that money.

Case V: Miss Y.—Miss Y. spent her youth in a large house in the country, and when conditions forced her to come to the city and get a job, she found the first year hard to take. Her most bitter loss, she decided, was her garden, on which she had spent a great deal of time and lavished affection. After thinking the matter over through a siege of wakeful nights, she made up her mind that she would have a garden regardless. With this idea to the fore, she started apartment hunting and kept right on till she found a one-room affair, which was adequate and not too expensive and which had long windows opening onto a small tin roof. Her announcement that she proposed to turn this unpromising area into a garden met with derision on the part of her friends, who evidently didn't know Miss Y. as well as they thought.

We are not prepared to say how her ends were accomplished, but eventually the tin roof blossomed like an oasis and even the skylight that erupted in the center disappeared under a trellis of ivy. Since the roof will accommodate two garden chairs, and no more, and has a romantic glamour on a moonlit night, we feel that Miss Y.'s investment in good earth and green plants may prove to be profitable.

Case VI: Miss E.—Miss E. is a Maiden Lady with all the characteristics the term implies. She believes implicitly that everything about the Good Old Days was infinitely superior to anything about the present, and her life is one long unsuccessful struggle to preserve the past intact. She lives in the house in which she was born, in a once-stylish neighborhood now inhabited by people with all sorts of odd backgrounds, and she keeps everything in the exact spot where her mother set it as a bride, at least fifty years ago.

If Miss E.'s income was all that it once was, this story would be sad enough, but added acidity enters with the fact that her income is one of the things she has not been able to preserve in its original state. While it would do nicely for an enterprising woman in a small up-to-date apartment, it is sadly inadequate for a rambling house needing a ton of coal a week in winter weather and several servants in any weather. Miss E. has no servants, and both she and the house look it. The wallpaper is peeling in the drawing room, the sofa springs are sagging, the plumbing is temperamental, and even Miss E.'s Sunday black has a rusty tinge.

Miss E. has all the earmarks of a Collector's Item, but she is an item that nobody wants to collect.

Case VII: Mrs. G.—Mrs. G., as she will tell you herself, has a perfect husband and four remarkable children. Until recently, Mr. G. worked for a firm that was glad to pay him more than enough to support a good-sized and expensively decorated house in a smart suburb and send all the children to the best school. But Mr. G. had ambitions, the chief of which was to have his own business— a desire that could be attained only by drastic measures, including Cutting Down on Everything.

That being the case, Mrs. G. decided philosophically that she could Cut Down as well as the next person, if not a little better, and why not? On looking around, she felt that she could, in fact, do quite a lot better. And she did.

She began by moving the family to a large frame house of the mid-McKinley period, which was definitely in the country (though not too far for Mr. G. to commute to town) and in inconvenient and not smart country at that. While she realizes the advantages of good Environment, she feels that there are several varieties of good environment, and the new place exemplifies one of them, especially while the children are young. They go to public school by bus, and while their schoolmates are not dressed by De Pinna, their studying of reading, writing, and arithmetic is not interrupted by making costumes for the school plays or pintrays out of pewter.

Mrs. G. came to the conclusion, early in the game, that an old frame house was not the place for Dignified Elegance—not this old frame house, at any rate. She therefore went in for Colorful Gaiety, much of which she has herself supplied with a paintbrush (with some aid from the older children, acquired by the Tom Sawyer method). The dining room woodwork is now a very pale yellow, and the insides of the built-in corner cupboards are turquoise blue. Mrs G. keeps yellow flowering plants in turquoise blue pots (painted with leftover paint) on the windowsills. The wide boards of the floor in the smaller living room, used as a library and game room, are painted red, under the dark brown rug, and she has made slip covers for the two big chairs out of Turkey-red flannel.

Crisp white argentine curtains in the master bedroom are tied back with field flowers from the discount store, and Mrs. G.'s dressing table is covered with white argentine, which sheds dust as a duck sheds water.

Mrs. G.'s final triumph was in the large living room, where the mirror on the mantel was cracked. She persuaded Mr. G. to take it down and remove the old walnut frame, and then she cut out an enchanting design from one roll of imported toile de Jouey wallpaper, pasted it on the mirror (and over the crack), had a glazier cut a piece of clear glass to fit over it, and had the whole thing framed in a narrow apple-green frame to match the sateen curtains. The effect made up for the day the furnace didn't work and the morning the water froze in the kitchen pipes.

Mrs. G., stimulated by the fact that the children are having an elegant time, is pretty proud of her accomplishments. She sometimes wonders how she kept herself amused when someone else did all the interesting things for her.

CHAPTER THREE

PLEASE DRESS

ONE THING that practically every woman we ever met believes in her heart is that she has really remarkable taste in clothes and could look like a million dollars if she had the million or the time. She may know that, actually, she looks like a country cousin nine days out of ten and occasionally slips into the cartoon class, but it doesn't alter her conviction. That is, she feels, the fault of Circumstance. Fate has given her other, more important things on which to spend her money, or she has too much to do. Or maybe she's too intellectual. Anyway, it isn't that she doesn't know.

We're willing to wager that it is just that. The women who know *do* look like a million dollars and often they do it on very little money. We admit that it takes a certain amount of time (you seldom get anything for nothing in this vale of tears), but it's worth spending time on. You've got to wear clothes whether you like them or not, unless you want to join a Nudist Colony or go to jail, and wearing the right clothes makes life a lot simpler. If you don't wear the right clothes, the ones you do choose will wear on you—not to mention your embarrassed family.

Fashion sense is a gift vouchsafed to a favored few, like a talent for music or sculpture, but anyone can acquire adequate fashion knowledge, and it will prove to be an economy, as well as an aid in getting jobs, invitations, and beaux, and adding enormously to your peace of mind. Very few women have a mind above clothes when they find themselves in conspicuous places, and those who have make their families wish they hadn't. (If this seems flippant, just remember how many occasions there are when a noble nature and a beautiful disposition don't show, but an unbecoming hat and a slip below your hem do.)

The truth of the matter is (though a surprising number of women overlook it) that most people have to put in a little thought and study in order to look as well as they should. There are a few good rules that they ought to learn and that we are going to enlarge on at any moment, but even these aren't enough. The rules hold good from season to season, but fashions go right on changing. It isn't enough either to notice that they're wearing a lot of artichoke green this year, or elephant gray, and to run out and get a green or gray dress.

Knowing your fashions, or at least knowing the elementary points about them, is the first and greatest economy and one that two women out of three skip entirely. They are serenely unconscious of the fact that if they would buy a few issues of the most authoritative fashion magazines every spring and fall, and read these issues from cover to cover in the spirit of a student studying a textbook the night before examination, they'd save twice as much money as they do by bargain hunting. (If you *must* bargain hunt, do it late in the season at a good shop; not early in the season at a cheap one.)

A new mode is a complicated thing. It's made up of colors and fabrics and skirt lengths and waist lengths and relative proportions and a hundred details. The untrained woman's eye doesn't take them in at a glance. As a matter of fact, she doesn't have to take them all in, but she ought to take in more than she does. What usually happens is that a dress or a suit or a coat that is new in every detail looks pretty funny to her. "That," she thinks, "would be fine for Miss Ina Claire or Mrs. Harrison Williams, but I'd look as if I'd gone a little mad if I should wear it." She may be right. But she's not right when, instead, she buys a dress that, in all but one or two new points, has all the familiarity of a dear old family friend. She'll enjoy wearing it for about six weeks and then, lunching at the country club, she'll feel suddenly dowdy beside Mrs. Smith's smart little number.

Or maybe you belong to the other school, which loves a change and rushes out to buy a couple of models in the first spring crop. These usually give you a fine fresh-as-a-daisy feeling the first times you wear them and a terrible pain later on.

It's a lot wiser to follow the Fashion Girls, whose business it is to know What's What, which things will spread over the country like an epidemic and eventually make you just as sick, and which will be gone with the wind before you've had enough wear out of them to pay for the alterations. They've put everything down in black and white (to say nothing of the elegant color printing in all our best publications) and you can get the benefit merely by stopping at the nearest newsstand. It may not seem very enlightening as you read, but the sum total of information you should glean will save you from buying a lot of clothes that have passed the peak of chic and are just about to start sliding.

The basic rules behind any smart budget wardrobe may be pretty old, but they've got a lot of wear in them yet. There's the old saw (tell us if you haven't heard this one before) about building your wardrobe around one color. You may have learned that one just after the alphabet, but if you always follow it, you're a stronger-minded woman than most. It's amazing, in this enlightened age, to see how many women will go out and buy a brown coat, just as they planned to do, and then get carried away by a little navy blue dress that is too sweet, and eventually choose a black hat because they can't find a becoming one in any other color and black goes with everything. (Oh, does it?) Once you've done that, you can choose between wearing all three and looking as if you didn't know any better or getting three complete outfits. We wouldn't know which to advise.

Sticking to one color isn't the only grim necessity, either, if you really mean economy. It's got to be a dark, practical, unoriginal color. To be explicit, it's got to be black or blue or brown. Not for you are the "dee-vine" new peanut butter tans or the passionate pansy purples or the whoopla reds. Not in your suits and dresses, at any rate.

Those little whimsies are for the girls with rich husbands, or something, and we hope they like them. But you will be a great deal happier if you start with a coat that isn't something to remember you by. A coat that is a smart, trim, inconspicuous background for less expensive flights of fancy.

What's more, you'd better get your hats and shoes, your bags (or some of them if you have several), and most of your dresses in the same unexciting shade. It may sound monotonous, but it's the greatest single economy there is, when it comes to clothes. With this plan, everything goes with everything else, as you should have discovered for yourself long before we thought of writing this book. Besides, there are still blouses and jackets and scarfs and belts and jewelry and handkerchiefs, among other trifles, to bring brightness into your sartorial life. With these and a little ingenuity, you ought to be able to be as gay or as striking or as appealing as any lady should be.

A good second rule is never to buy clothes that are too definitely one-purpose clothes or even one-season clothes. Every garment in a small wardrobe should be able to go a lot of places. Those cheery sports coats that reek of the heather are all very chic for Lady Who-Are-You, who has eight or ten coats in her closet, but you and I will come out better with a simple wool model that can double for motoring or travel or rainy days or shopping in town. And you ought to be able to track down some dresses, also simple, of good enough lines and materials to go unblushingly to any tea, without making you look All Dressed Up at lunch, or even at a typewriter. You ought, too, to stay away from conspicuous clothes, which may be alluring the first couple of months, but not in their second year. A wisp of satin and a red cyclamen worn over your right eye as a hat has charm only when you know there is some less fancy millinery waiting in your closet. And an evening frock cut like a dirndl is amusing only if you don't have to wear it too often.

Beware the velvet and organdy evening frocks, too, or any others that you can't wear the year around in a pinch. They may be enchanting, but they are extravagances in a budgeted wardrobe. A really limited wardrobe shouldn't have more than one formal evening dress anyway, and that should have a jacket that can be worn or left at home. Social life has gone so chatty that there are now twenty occasions when a dinner frock is more appropriate than bare-backed formality, to one that demands the other, more elegant variety. (Bare-backed formality, incidentally, was never very becoming to any but the young and beautiful.)

We don't know how frugal you want to be, but if clothes are a problem at best, just apply this betwixt-and-between principle to everything. A hat that is about halfway between a golfing model and an evening creation is your best bet. (A hat that exactly matches your coat, of course, and that goes with all of your dresses.)

This may sound unexciting, but as a matter of fact, you can be just as chic in an outfit that doesn't tell where you're going as in one that does. And don't think that we are urging a wardrobe that isn't the last word in flattery as well as smartness. The beau-catching clothes are not necessarily the ones that cause the heads to turn on the street. You might follow every rule in this chapter and still be a Glamour Girl, and we hope you will.

We aren't going to make out a budget or even a plan. Budgets usually presuppose that you are, as the lady in the play wanted to be, naked with a checkbook. We know there must be women in this enviable predicament—shipwrecked heroines or women whose houses burn to the ground in the night, leaving them in a pink silk nightie—but we've never happened to meet one. The problems with which we are most familiar have to do with building a wardrobe around last year's slightly worn coat and a couple of old dresses, and making it all look as Parisian as possible, or at any rate as much like Fifty-Seventh Street, New York, as we know how.

As for the list of clothes—that should be based on age, size, type, locality, what you do all day, and with whom you do it. We might plan fifty and still not hit every one. Besides, we hope that this little guidebook with be a staff for you to lean on for years to come, but our pet theories (like having a skirt in the color of your topcoat made on a bodice top to go under several gay contrasting jackets) might be as smart as paint this year, but by next year we may all be wearing shawls or smocks instead of jackets. We don't claim to be a prophet.

We still have some rules up our sleeve, however. One is to make a plan of your spring and autumn purchases before you buy so much as a boutonniere, and then stick to it. This is another old adage that goes right on being true, like a Bible quotation. But it takes a lot of character to carry it out, in the face of the semiannual crop of temptations. Public opinion to the contrary, the really well-dressed woman is either rich or a lady of unswerving principle and willpower.

Most of us might have made out a list something like the following, this spring:

• Toast-brown wool coat, untrimmed. Simple and

well-cut. Warm enough to wear through next autumn, and a good model to wear with separate furs.

- Black silk crepe dress. (With brown suede belt. To go under coat.)

- Black sheer wool dress. (With brown wood buttons. Also to wear under coat.)

- Short toast-brown wool jacket. (Lightweight. To wear over either black dress and with separate skirt.)

- Checked brown-and-black-and-white light wool skirt.

- Printed silk dress. (With brown and white in design; to be worn under coat or without it.)

- Toast-brown hat, bag, and shoes.

- Lighter brown gloves and stockings.

- White gloves, bag or hat, and jacket. (Warm-weather accessories. Jacket to go with separate skirt or over print dress. Bag or hat and gloves to go with print.)

This is a good, workable plan with plenty of variety for all the daytime activities of the average person, even if she's as busy as Mrs. Roosevelt. But does that same average person end up with anything remotely resembling her original plan? She does not. The results of a few strenuous shopping sessions are much more likely to be something like this:

- Toast-brown wool coat, with brown fur collar. (This will look too warm in hot weather, and it won't be smart with the print dress. The fur seems good, but can't be at the price. But it was the most becoming model she had found on Tuesday afternoon, after two days of shopping, and she simply *had* to have a new coat for Mrs. Montmorency's party on Wednesday.)

- Black silk crepe dress. (With white lingerie touch at the neckline. This won't look well under the coat, and it will be a lot of trouble to keep clean, but perhaps it won't show much and she can rip it off later.)

- Black sheer wool dress. (With silver buttons. She can change these to the brown wooden ones she'd planned, but ten chances to one she won't.)

- Short red jacket. (This was so smart she just couldn't resist it. It will look all right with the black dresses, probably, if she gets out last year's black hat and has it steamed. But what about shoes and bag?)

- Navy blue printed ensemble. (This cost scarcely a cent more than she'd planned to spend on the brown-and-white skirt, which she won't get now that she has a red jacket instead of a brown one. And maybe she can save somewhere else and get both a white bag and a white hat. Or maybe she can't.)

- Printed silk dress. (With bright flowers on a black ground. Very fresh and springlike, and *so* flattering. But she won't be able to wear it under the coat.)

This brings us to Mrs. Average Person's accessories—and what to do? Brown ones won't look well with the black dresses she's bought, unless she ties them together with a change of trimming—a lot of trouble and a needless expense. And they won't look right with the printed dress or the navy blue ensemble anyway. Black ones won't be very smart with her coat. Navy blue ones would be dowdy with any of her purchases except the navy blue outfit. We're glad that it's her problem and not ours, but we're willing to wager that she solves it by getting two sets, both cheaper than she'd planned and both doomed to look it in about six weeks. Accessories are *not* the place to do the heaviest economizing.

That gloomy little discourse leads us back to the well-known fact that the most expensive item in your wardrobe and the greatest extravagance is the garment that can't be worn with a lot of other things (also in your wardrobe) or that you seldom wear at all, because you don't like it. If you have to economize, you can't afford mistakes, which are definitely luxuries.

Another good rule is not to attempt to have everything come within the same price range. Buy a coat or suit or street dress at a more expensive shop than your budget would allow if you averaged things up, and make up for it in the clothes you wear around the house and in your evening wardrobe.

A lot of dresses sold under the unbeguiling name of housedresses are good, trim little models with simple lines and no gewgaws, and they could understudy some of the wool and cotton sports clothes sold at eight or ten times their price without being suspected. They probably do, more often than you or I guess. There are, of course, plenty of house-frock atrocities too, but it's up to you to know one from the other. One type will give you that determinedly simple, Boston-aristocrat look; the other suggests a frowsy, inadequate housewife in a far from elegant flat.

As for your evening clothes—here is a place where variety is more important than wearing qualities anyway. You probably don't wear out one evening frock a year— really wear it out—and nobody wants to go to too many parties in the same old dress. Smart lines and becoming colors that give an effect, even if they don't last, will do as much toward keeping you from being a wallflower as a two-hundred-dollar dress, though we wouldn't turn up our nose at the two-hundred-dollar dress if we could have one, which seems improbable.

The Little Black Evening Dress is, of course, the great standby of nine-tenths of the economically minded women in the country, and it has done its part nobly for a couple of decades. It doesn't soil easily, isn't remembered like a color, is appropriate anywhere, and can be varied by contrasting jackets, jewels, flowers, scarfs, and slippers till it dies on its feet. The idea may not excite you, but if you're really going in for saving money, you'd better get one anyway. In a few short months, you'll probably love it like a sister, though you would be heartily sick of anything else. No less practical is the long black evening wrap, and you needn't be ashamed to get this in the cheapest store you can find that carries evening wraps. We mean cheap too. Those serve-yourself emporiums, for instance, often have simple ones (those of wool or a heavy silk faille are usually more satisfactory than those of cheap velvet) which, wrapped around your slender form in a theater lobby or even the country club dressing room, won't look very different from the costly one on your neighbor, and the difference may be in your favor.

It is now our stern duty, however, to say a few sharp words against too casual buying of cheap clothes. We don't say that it can't be done with triumphant results, but we do say that it offers a lot of temptations to get a dress or a coat with just a teeny-weeny bit too much trimming, or lines the faintest shade too extreme, or some other detail that is almost but not quite right. If the rhinestone buckle with too large stones doesn't come off, if the cut is a hint too-too and the success of the alterations is questionable, it isn't a good buy. And never, never get a dress that is a bit skimpy. It won't wear, and it won't look right even when it's new, and though you may plan to reduce, there is always the chance that you'll add a few pounds instead.

An excellent economy, incidentally, is to keep thin. We regret as much as you do that every pound over your ideal weight is a strain on your clothes, but it's true, and what's more, it's the thin girls who get the bargains in the first place. Those elegant little models that you see in shop windows for next to nothing always turn out to be in the very small sizes.

If you are frankly overweight and still must buy bargains, get them a shade large and have them fitted. The additional wear will more than pay for the cost of alterations, and you'll look a lot better besides. Fitting, by the way, is a much-neglected art. Too many women buy a dress in the size nearest their figure and wear it as is, wondering why it looks only so-so. Often, a slightly raised waistline or shoulder line will make an inexpensive model look like three times the price, and the lack of it will do the reverse. Especially the shoulder line. Well-fitted shoulders have chic that is authoritative.

The real clothes economists are, of course, the ones who Make Things Last without looking it. The French lead all the rest in this respect, one reason being that they take off their street clothes practically on crossing their own thresholds and would no more loll in a broadcloth suit than they would wear it to do the family washing. They get into those little house frocks we've already eulogized or into one of the tea gowns that can make you feel more elegant on less money than any other garment. But they

don't relax—not until they've brushed the street costume spotless and put it on a hanger that will really keep it in shape. We don't mean just any wire hanger; we mean what we said.

This matter of caring for the clothes you have could be the subject of a whole sermon on economy. Brushing and cleaning and pressing and putting things away properly may be drab activities, but they pay and pay and pay. The most expensive dress is a sorry sight if it's wrinkled, and we hesitate even to bring up the matter of spots. But a crisp, fresh, immaculate look is attractive and chic in itself. Amateur cleaning is, however, a doubtful economy, unless you have the gift. Many is the time we've started with the best of intentions and ended with the original spot, an additional ring, and a temper. Our advice is to include a small sum for cleaning in your monthly budget and not attempt the next-to-impossible. Incidentally, it's a good idea not to make the sum *too* small, if that can be avoided, since the not-too-cheap cleaners are apt to be worth the extra price.

But this doesn't let you out of brushing your hats and your frocks and your shoes (and not all with the same brush, either). Or of putting trees in your shoes the minute you take them off, and hustling them to the shoemaker at the first sign of a run-down heel or a scuffed toe; or of wrapping metal cloth slippers in black flannel, and putting hats on stands on the closet shelf, and light evening dresses under argentine cloth covers, and artificial flowers in boxes, and sweaters in drawers. It's all pretty wearing, we admit, but it will save you enough for an extra new dress or maybe a weekend Away From It All. Anyway, if you have a really small wardrobe, everything has to be ready all of the time, and it won't be unless you follow the rules.

We're going to condense the rest of our theories into a few short (well, fairly short) maxims. There's just a chance that you'll remember some of them.

- Don't buy clothes to wear to the places you'd like to go (like a garden party, if you live in the city, or an outdoor horse show); buy them to wear to the places you do go.

- Don't keep on wearing what was becoming ten years ago; fashions have changed and so have your hair, skin, and figure.

- In assembling a smart wardrobe, you have to spend *something*—money, time, or taste.

- Three black dresses in a row in your closet won't bore you one quarter as much as three in any other color.

- Women who say they can't be bothered about clothes are bothered as much as anyone else when they find themselves wearing a dowdy costume in a group of well-dressed women. Inexpensive clothes can often be made to last as long as expensive ones, given the same care (not almost the same care).

- Dressing smartly doesn't necessarily mean dressing dramatically. It's just as smart to be conservatively well dressed, and a lot more women who try it look like ladies.

- Don't try to be a "type" on a limited income. Going Spanish or Directoire or Victorian is expensive, and while a bonnet and a bang may be chic this year, the chances are that they'll look like fancy-dress in another season.

- Beware of the surplice dress, especially after forty. It's a superbly cut surplice that doesn't add a few years to the age of the wearer.

- A cheap dress worn with good accessories will fool more people than an expensive dress worn with cheap accessories.

- A suit is the backbone of many a smart wardrobe, but not the most down-to-earth wardrobes. You have to have a coat anyway, and while both coat and suit are nice, it's not actually necessary to have both.

- Any wardrobe that hasn't at least one dress that makes you feel as pretty and as elegant as you can possibly feel is a washout.

CASES

Case VIII: Miss D.—Miss D. is an intelligent young woman whom necessity brought from a small town to a large city in search of a job. While learning her way around, she stayed at a girls' club where there were a number of other young women in the same position, and she soon noticed that several of them were meeting repeated rebuffs, while others got what they wanted with little or no difficulty. The first, it seemed to her, presented a pretty dilapidated appearance, but the second were dressed with a smartness that suggested efficiency, and she began to wonder if there wasn't a connection between clothes and getting a job. The more she thought about it, the more she felt that it might be hard to convince an employer that you had really remarkable brains if the brains weren't equal to assembling a reasonably up-to-date costume.

She, therefore, devoted her first ten days—and a proportion of her meager capital that would have seemed scandalous to her relatives at home—to getting together a small office wardrobe. She started with a navy blue three-piece costume that cost more than one-third of the money she had set aside for clothes. The topcoat was trim, well cut, high-shouldered, and good to wear with other things. The jacket and skirt could be worn as a dress or a suit, with only a gilet added, in or out of the office. An additional navy blue dress, classically simple and with sleeves almost to the elbows, was her only other large purchase, but she spent a lot of time on her accessories. These included a canary yellow gilet and gloves, to go with the suit; a rose red suede belt to wear with the dress and a grosgrain hat band that matched and could go on her blue felt hat; a blue-and-white checked jacket to go with the suit skirt and a rose red carnation to wear with it; and a white piqué waistcoat blouse and white gloves. The carnation could go also on the topcoat when she wore it over the dress, and she bought a white carnation to wear with the white gloves with either the dress or the suit. These carnations, incidentally, were each made from two purchased at the discount store and bound together to look like one.

Miss D. wore her three-piece costume, complete with the yellow accessories, when she started job hunting. At the first place, she sat for twenty minutes in the reception room between two other applicants—a girl with a flower-print dress with magenta in the design, under a brown tweed coat, and a second girl in a fancy knitted outfit combining black, white, and turquoise blue, with short sleeves and worn with a bonnetlike black hat.

Miss D. got the job.

Case IX: Mrs. X.—Mrs. X. is an attractive wife in a charming suburb, but she lives the life of a chauffeur. She taxies her husband to the train, her children to school, her oldest son to Boy Scout meetings and her daughter to dancing lessons, herself to social engagements, and the dog to the veterinary's. She also does the marketing by car, does social-service work in it once a week, and collects her husband from the station every night.

Mrs. X. discovered some time ago that while her health bore up under the strain, her clothes didn't. At first, she tried to solve the problem by wearing old clothes, but she wore them so much of the time that she soon felt like a charity orphan. She therefore had a really smart coat made out of tweed with as ironlike qualities as she could find, which can rub against the steering wheel without disaster through her innumerable exits and entrances and will stand endless strain on the shoulders. She also has special driving gloves and heavy low-heeled sports shoes, both of which have their own sturdy chic.

This has tripled the wear of the rest of Mrs. X.'s wardrobe. She wears her car clothes whenever she can, and when she goes to a party on the same trip with some taxiing, she changes gloves, shoes, and coat in the car or lets somebody else do the driving.

Case X: Mrs. R.—Mrs. R. is a professor's wife, who doesn't like to fuss about her clothes. She has too good a mind, however, not to know that a dowdy appearance is as much of a handicap as a crippled leg and not so unavoidable. She, therefore, worked out a plan several seasons ago, which she still follows with pleasure and profit.

She had the best pattern firm she could find cut and fit a muslin pattern of a shirtwaist dress with the lines of the current mode, and then she had an excellent "little dressmaker" make it up in several different fabrics—wool cashmere and linen for daytime, silk crepe for afternoon, lamé and chiffon for evening. The evening models had long skirts and buttonholes to hold some lovely jewelled studs, but were identical with the daytime models in every other particular.

The style is extremely becoming to Mrs. R., and the plan needs little thought and next to no fitting. She is wise enough, however, to have a new pattern made each season, with such details as shoulder line, waistline, skirt fullness, and length exactly right for the newest mode. This keeps her from being dowdy or arty, and while most women would find the scheme monotonous, it is entirely satisfactory to Mrs. R.

Case XI: Miss J.—Miss J. believes in putting her money into things that show, and is a passionate economizer in minor details. She has a half dozen small economies that save her enough to allow considerable splurging in more spectacular ways. She buys cheap evening slippers, for instance, and never has more than two pairs at once—one black and one gold or silver. These go with all her evening clothes, which are planned with that in mind, and since, as she says, she doesn't hike when she's all dressed up, they last well enough for the things she does do.

She also makes it a rule never, even in an emergency, to buy less than six pairs of stockings at once, so that she can remate pairs when a single stocking goes back on her. (She feels that a full dozen pairs are even better, but she can't always finance so many.)

Miss J. has learned, with some difficulty, to manicure her own nails successfully—a great saving—and she experimented till she found a good but inexpensive face cream that agrees with her skin. She buys it in the largest jars available and uses it with regularity.

Another pet economy practiced by this efficient young woman is the purchase of plain, well-made, tailored underwear, which costs a little less and lasts a great deal longer than lace-trimmed or hemstitched models. She insists on good lines, however, so that when she catches a glimpse of herself partly dressed, in the long mirror on her closet door, her morale doesn't drop.

She also sticks to white for all summer sports and country clothes, and wears washable white summer accessories and removable white trimmings whenever possible. She has found that white doesn't fade, it doesn't go out of fashion, it washes better than anything else, and her white dresses combine with all sorts of coats, hats, and accessories, including the dark basic color of her current wardrobe.

Miss J.'s final economy is to buy coats that are completely minus tricks or passing fads in cut and trimming—models so classic, in fact, that they are as smart in their third or fourth year as on the day she bought them. She now has a tweed sports coat of a cut that is practically timeless, and a velvet evening wrap that she's worn five years, and a coat from last spring that looks like this spring. With this substantial framework, she feels that she's entitled to something slightly whoopsy-doopsy every now and then.

Case XII: Miss M.—Miss M. had a prosperous girlhood during which she showed a streak of minor miserliness that has since proved invaluable. She hoarded all the good-looking buckles, buttons, belts, and clips on her expensive clothes, wrapping them in tissue paper and keeping them in a box as carefully as though they were family heirlooms.

Recently, the complete evaporation of her income has made it necessary for Miss M. to go to work and also to wear inexpensive clothes, but her friends can't imagine where she finds such handsome ones for what she can afford. As a matter of fact, they are no handsomer than theirs. It's the trimmings, dug out of Miss M.'s precious box and put on in place of the original ones, that do the trick.

Case XIII: Mrs. F.—When Mr. F. died, after a long illness that used up most of the life insurance, Mrs F. did not think, "Dear, dear, what shall I do?" She thought, "Well, well, what can I do?" Her problem was complicated by two young children, but she soon got an answer.

She could knit. She could knit fast and well, and she does knit as many hours out of her twenty-four as is possible, which is more than you think. She knits all her own dresses except those she wears in the evening, and most of the children's clothes. (Incidentally, she has begun to knit for her friends, and she now has several women who knit for her by the hour, following her excellent designs, and has built up a small business that shows signs of growing into a much larger one.)

Case XIV: Miss W.—Miss W. is a businesswoman who feels that she can't spend much on her evening clothes but who wants to look as well as the next when she does go out in the evening. Her solution of that little poser is one beautifully cut black evening dress and several changes of accessories. At the moment, the dress is the background for:

- An emerald green taffeta jacket and emerald green slippers.

- Two handsome ruby red clips and a bracelet to match, worn with black slippers and bag.

- Some handsome shaded pink chiffon roses and a pink chiffon handkerchief, worn with the black slippers and bag.

- A gold lamé jacket and gold bag, also worn with the black slippers.

If Miss W.'s black dress still looks as smart next season as she thinks it will, she won't get another, but will get a black sequin jacket instead, and perhaps another change in some bulky gold jewelry that will serve later on a simple black daytime dress.

CHAPTER FOUR

CAN YOU AFFORD A HUSBAND?

WELL, CAN you? A lot of women do, and support them nicely on a small salary at that. And why not, if they want to? It may be an extravagance, but even periods of strict economy should include some extravagances if possible. The best-planned budgets are not those that are the most drably practical; they are the ones that give the budgeteers the best run for their money.

One of the things that has made economy so unpopular is that people are apt to practise it with grim determination. Too many economizers, in our opinion, go in for Keeping Up a Front, with only the bare necessities behind the front. We are all for taking down the front and using its upkeep to get more fun out of living.

One of the most popular narcotics to ease the pain of economy is cherishing the belief that better days are ahead. This is both efficacious and commendable, but it sometimes turns out to be a habit-forming drug. The addicts keep pushing off their spending days, which is bad for their dispositions and hard on their families and friends. Even during emergencies when you need the dose, you shouldn't take it in large enough quantities to dull the consciousness that your better days may be too far ahead to be of much use to you. Things to which you look forward too long are almost invariably disappointing when you get them, and you *might* die first anyway.

Besides, though it's both wise and courageous to live in the future now and then, it never gets you entirely away from the present. The present, like the poor, is always with you, and every miserable day you let yourself endure is a large enough proportion of your life to be worth salvaging. You may be one of those people who have to do a good deal of economizing a good part of your life (there are enough of them to win any election) and if you settle back and do it gloomily, your sum total of fun will be pretty meager. This is unnecessary and not very enterprising.

The chances are that you can have at least part of the things you want most, whatever your income, and the intelligent economizer figures out what it is that he or she really wants. (It is seldom the first thing that comes into your head.)

But it might be a husband. And if the one you have in mind is, like so many eligible and charming men, a non-money-maker and you still prefer him to a larger apartment or a trip to Europe—why not take him on? It is your affair. (And his; we are assuming that he, though unprofitable, is not unwilling.) A part of small, as well as large, sums of money should be invested in happiness. And, even leaving out the over-written question of Love, it is perfectly understandable that any woman should like to have a man to sit at the head of her table when she entertains, and make a fourth at bridge, and go to the theater with her, and open the gingerale bottles, and get out the ice cubes.

It is a regrettable, but undeniable, fact that the most delightful people are seldom big money-makers. A few may have inherited large incomes, but they generally lose them or spend them. Getting rich is apt to be a twenty-four-hour-a-day job and not always worth the trouble. It leaves little time for the arts and graces, without a few of which most people are pretty trying.

This has always been admitted in high-minded moments (like church and first meetings with mothers-in-law). In fact, some of the best Famous Quotations we know are based on the idea. But until the Depression remolded current opinion in so many ways, it was more theory than anything else. If you wanted to be Somebody, you began by trying to roll up a bank account, and if you couldn't, it was just too bad. (Geniuses were excepted, but usually not till they were dead.) We then went through a few years in which Somebodies, judged by these standards, were as rare as chinchilla coats, and a lot of the few who did stand out were women. Things finally came to such a pass that even Society admitted that Nice People were often poor.

We have reviewed this bit of history because of its pleasantly upsetting effect. It brought in the Smart Poor, who are both newer and more numerous than the nouveau riche, and far more amusing. Once, you could be poor and genteel, but not poor and smart. (The few exceptions were practically freaks of nature, like Siamese twins and quintuplets.) And as that type of gentility is an elegant quality that nobody wants, it was usual to conceal all signs of poverty to the last silver spoon.

The Smart Poor do not pretend to be rich, which makes everything different. Once you give up struggling to fool people, you can have a lot more fun on very little money.

You can live in a funny flat in a poor city neighborhood or a remodeled barn in the country. You can go to cheap foreign cinemas and boast about it, instead of skimping in order to be seen at the Opera. You can hunt up bargains in clothes and rip off the gewgaws and—if you have the flair and the figure—look like a million dollars. And on the other hand, you can buy orchids when you need a new rug and, if you feel like it, get yourself a husband instead of a bank account.

The point, nowadays, is not merely to know the cost of a thing and whether you have money to pay for it, but to know whether it's worth the price to you. An expensive coat may be a paying investment because of its chic and its wearing qualities, and an inexpensive one may be an extravagance you shouldn't indulge in for the same reasons reversed. It is even possible that you'll be wise to get the expensive coat, just for the kick you'd get out of it.

Knowing what you are getting for your money and how much you'll like it when you get it is particularly important when personal relationships are involved. Can we, or can we not, afford to marry—on the man's salary or the man's plus the woman's?—This is a subject of chronic debate as violent as the seething over the Supreme Court issue, and half the debaters get the wrong answer. They do their computing on a purely dollar-and-cent basis and don't stop to figure out what they want out of marriage anyway and whether it's all in the budget. If your picture of being a wife is pretty luxurious, that's an item you'd better put down right after Rent and Food, and then see whether you can cut down somewhere else. If the man's idea of romance is built round a chic figure with glamorous clothes and lily white hands, you'd better be pretty sure that one of you can pay for them.

On the other hand, if affection and companionship are worth more to you than trimmings (which is the most satisfactory state of affairs), you are foolish not to take the Leap as soon as possible, and we hope it will be within a couple of weeks or, at most, months after you make the great decision. Health and enthusiasm and energy and common sense and imagination can all go on the asset side of your budget, and more than half the things brides once thought were necessities can be left off entirely. Hope chests

have been shrinking, and Setting Up Housekeeping is a lot sketchier than it used to be. Gone are the days when any self-respecting bride had linen enough to last a lifetime.

If you do take the Step, don't do it with the notion that you're giving up a lot and that this shows a noble nature. All it shows is that you thought you would like what you got better than what you gave up, which is probably true. As for appreciation—before you demand too much, you might remember that your husband gave up something too, and he has his own moments of wistful memories. Bachelor days have an aura that is positively dazzling.

Those who are debating whether to go on working have at least one problem settled for them. They don't have to wonder whether it can be done successfully. The women who are doing it numbered something like ten and a half million the last time we saw the statistics and there are a lot more now. Those that we know are not overworked martyrs. They may be two-job women, but they like both jobs and have more fun out of each because of the variety. It's all a matter of apportioning your time efficiently. There are, after all, only twenty-four hours a day, and most interesting people are pantingly busy for as many of these hours as they are awake, which is all you can manage with one or ten jobs. In these labor-saving days, few women spend all of the hours in homemaking, even without a job—though it can be done.

Here, again, it's what you want out of life that ought to decide the matter. If you have the home-loving heart once so much lauded, and would rather picture yourself in crisp little house frocks than in tailored suits, or if your husband's idea of a perfect wife is a little woman who knows how to make apple pie and knows very little else, you'd better give up your job tomorrow, if not today. (And we're not denying that a lot of men with this idea are still extant.) But if you like more trimmings than your husband's salary will cover, and believe that they will pay in happiness for him as well as you, keep the job or get a new one.

Of course, you may *have* to keep it in order to get married at all, but don't worry too much, even though you are one of the Homebodies. Our personal opinion is that the average wage-earning woman is more interesting and keeps younger and handsomer than if she stayed home, whether she really likes working or not. We can cite as many exceptions to this as you can, but we still think it's true in the main. And ten chances to one, she's a marvellous housekeeper besides, or a good enough one at the very least. The notion that offices kill the domestic instinct hasn't a leg to stand on. They foster it. To the average woman who works in an office, home has the charm, if not the glory, of the not-too-familiar. It is the place where she can relax, and have fun, and do what she pleases. Even the work she does there becomes an adventure, because she has to make time for it and never gets quite as much done as she'd like to (though she manages to get enough done). She is apt to have even more pride in it than the woman who stays there more constantly, and all the eating she has to do in restaurants usually makes her much more sophisticated about food than her stay-at-home sisters.

We ourselves have run our one-woman ménage both with and without an office job, and our testimony is that we do it as thoroughly (and more gaily) before nine o'clock, during an occasional lunch hour, after five-thirty, and over the weekend than we do when we devote full time to it. And it's a much more glamorous place when we have to leave it every morning.

But, to change our tune, you'd better be sure your job is really an asset and not a liability. There are plenty of women who nobly go off to work and whose jobs cost them more than their pay. When you go to an office, you have to have more town clothes (which cost much more than the clothes you could wear at home), and you probably have to have more service, and you certainly pay more for lunches. When an out-of-town cousin turns up, you undoubtedly entertain her more lavishly than if you could ask her to tea at home, and if you have children, the additional expenses roll up like a snowball.

And it's a rare working woman who doesn't feel justified in splurging every now and then, which is usually pretty often.

Even so, we are all for the job if you like it and can afford it. But be honest about your budgeting. Even a pretty good position can come into the orchid class, if you let it, and you'll come out better if you face this to start with.

Incidentally, it's improbable that you'll need to worry about objections on the part of your husband. He may be full of chivalrous notions about pouring riches into your lap, during the honeymoon, but he knows too that they are part of a fairy-story out of the past. Men have always expected women to work for them, and modern ones have next to no trouble in transposing the workroom from home to office. The trouble comes when you outdo them in success, especially in their own field; but if you're smart enough for that, you'll probably know how to meet the problem.

There's still another problem that puzzles a lot of people—whether a baby will come within the budget. Our sentimental advice is to have one anyway, if you want one and have been through the marriage ceremony. The people who wait till they can afford a baby seldom have one at all except by surprise. And it's not actually necessary to have it at the fanciest hospital, though we don't blame you for wanting to, or to have a layette from Paris. You may get satisfaction out of a bassinet trimmed with real lace, but the baby will never know the lace is there, and the same theory applies to a lot of things on baby budgets. People have perfectly healthy babies with very little money, no false pride, and the kind of courage to which we take off our hat.

CASES

Case XV: Mrs. P—Mrs. P. has an engrossing job as advertising manager of a large and ultra-smart shop, and she also has a husband and two very young daughters, all of whom she adores but doesn't see very much of. Her salary is large enough to be a problem when April fifteenth brings the income tax around, and her expenses are large enough to be a problem all of the time. She often wonders how in the world they would manage if she wasn't willing and able to go out into the world and earn as much as she does.

As she often explains, she really *has* to buy original French models in order to be well enough turned out for her position, and it's so much better for the children to live on Long Island that she has to have a car and chauffeur to get her into town. Obviously, since she can't be at home to supervise things, an experienced and reliable governess is a necessity, as is a well-trained butler to take some of the responsibility off her elegant white shoulders when she entertains.

Mr. P. does very well in a brokerage firm, but he couldn't quite manage all of these important items, Mrs. P. feels (with reason). Neither, to tell the truth, can Mrs. P. When she has paid for her clothes and her luncheons at the Colony Restaurant, where she entertains almost daily, and for the essential (and frequent) visits to the best beauty salon in town, and the annual trip to Europe that is so good for her work, there isn't much left for Long Island. The truth is that Mrs. P.'s job demands a lot of bubbly, and Mr. P. pays for it, but if he doesn't mind how much the job costs him, we don't know why we should either.

Case XVI: Mrs. B.—Mrs. B. hasn't been Mrs. B. very long, and in the business firm where she works (and has worked for eighteen years), she is still known as Miss X. She has a fair salary, but you would think she had much more than that. For Mrs. B. is a marvellous manager. Her living-room-bedroom-and-kitchenette apartment is attractively furnished; she always looks smartly, if simply, dressed; and she sees a few of the best plays and pictures and hears some of the best music and speeches. In addition to this, for years she has been putting something aside—not for a rainy day, but for a splurge.

She eventually made the splurge. She blew herself to a husband.

Mr. B. is a charming man, tall, handsome, and with knowledge of books, people, art, and the world in general. His conversational talents make him an asset at any party, and his disposition makes him an asset at home. But Mr. B. has never worked for more than a few consecutive weeks at any time in his life and then only when there was no possible way of avoiding it. He is a man who has Everything—or almost everything—except cash.

When Mrs. B.'s friends recovered from their intense surprise on hearing of the marriage of the level-headed Miss X., they settled down to head shaking. The poor dear, they said, had let herself in for something. She would have to support Mr. B. for the rest of her days.

Mrs. B. has every idea of supporting Mr. B. for the rest of her days and is delighted with the prospect. She realizes perfectly that he will require a lot of comforts, entertaining, and mothering, and she is confident that she can swing all of it and get her money's worth with interest. She adores going out with Mr. B.; she beams with pride when she introduces him as her husband; and she has never been so happy as in their companionship at home.

Case XVII: Mrs. C.—Mrs. C. is our idea of a heroine, not because of anything she does, but because she stays married to Mr. C. He has just had his fiftieth birthday and is earning considerably less than he did at forty-five. This, however, is not our grudge against him.

For the first fifteen years of their married life, Mr. C. plodded along, making enough money for them to live on comfortably, having enough friends, and believing that Success was just around the corner. He never did anything in particular about it, apparently thinking that success would come to him (and not that he should speed up a bit and overtake it). But a few years ago, he began to realize that he was no longer a young man getting experience for something Big. It even occurred to him that he had gone as far as he was going to get. There were two things, however, that didn't occur to him: First, that the lack was in him and he'd better overcome it (whatever it was) or else accept it. And second, that perhaps it didn't matter so much as he thought. That there might be something in the good old adage that money was not everything, since he had been perfectly happy to date, and so had Mrs. C.

Instead of this, Mr. C. went sour. He began to suspect that all his friends thought he was a failure. If they were particularly friendly, he thought they were sorry for him, and if they weren't, he thought they were snubbing him. He acquired a permanent chip on his shoulder, and his popularity began to dwindle.

It didn't take long for this to affect Mr. C.'s business relations, a field in which Getting On With People always plays so important a part. Eventually, Mr. C. was forced to make a change, and not for the better.

Mrs. C., who is a good sport, doesn't mind the difference in salary, but she does mind the difference in Mr. C.'s disposition. Evenings and weekends when they don't see their friends, he gets bored and sulky, and when they do see them, he gets offended and sullen. She is doing her best, which is very good indeed, but even a heroine can reach a limit.

In her place, we would give Mr. C. about six months more and then, if things hadn't improved, send him to a psychoanalyst or take a train to Reno.

Case XVIII: Mrs. N.—Mr. and Mrs. N. are one of those touching couples who have always wanted children Terribly and haven't any. Tears come to little Mrs. N.'s eyes whenever she refers to this.

Mr. N. works in a broker's office and Mrs. N. is an assistant to a smart decorator in Los Angeles. For the first eight years of their married life, the N.'s felt that they couldn't afford a baby. It took every cent of their combined salaries to pay for the six-room apartment, and the maid, and Getting Around as much as a young couple should, and Keeping Up with their Social Obligations.

Occasionally, they wondered if they might manage it, and then Mrs. N. would sit down with a pad and pencil and do a little figuring. The result was always a brand-new shock. Not only did it show that they couldn't possibly have a second maid, as she'd planned to do if her condition became Interesting, but it also showed that it would take several months for their combined salaries to pay up back bills. By that time, if a baby was imminent, she would have to buy baby clothes and bed jackets and the hospital expenses would be in the offing.

Eventually, Mrs. N. decided that she'd better have a baby soon if she was going to have one at all. In order to do it in proper style, she took on some extra work first, agreeing to decorate a couple of new houses in her evenings and over weekends. It was a very short time before she went to a hospital, but she had a nervous breakdown instead of a baby.

The doctor tells her that it would be inadvisable to have a baby at all, after so serious an illness, and Mrs. N. feels that she is a woman with a Great Sorrow, which makes her a very special person. She has never observed that nobody has everything.

CHAPTER FIVE

THINGS YOU CAN'T AFFORD

OF COURSE economizing is painful if you persist in applying it in the wrong places. You have to be careful where you pinch, though a lot of people just go ahead regardless. There are economies that nobody can afford unless they're so poor in purse and spirit that they don't care much anyway, and there are forms of thrift that are so expensive that not even a millionaire can pay for them.

First and foremost among these little errors is the extravagance of Letting Yourself Go. The woman who feels that she can't afford to keep herself as young, handsome, and chic as is humanly possible, or that she can do it just as well week after next when her finances are in better shape (only they may not be) eventually finds that she made a miscalculation that runs into money. The resulting debacle has been known to play havoc with both jobs and husbands, and it is bound to play havoc with her opinion of herself. In fact, there comes an inevitable day when she just can't stand herself As Is for another moment, and by that time the repairs are pretty expensive.

To make matters even worse for the married ladies, this illuminating hour often comes to them considerably later than it comes to their husbands, with unfortunate results. Lean periods are the times of all times to be as seductive as possible, since it's only normal for a man (or anybody else) to look around for an excuse for his difficulties, and a slovenly wife is as good an excuse as any other, if not a little better than most.

The wives have excuses too, of course, the most threadbare being that they haven't time. Economizing keeps them so frightfully busy. But since having plenty of money and all that goes with it also keeps women frightfully busy, and being in circumstances somewhere between the two takes time both ways, this excuse doesn't impress us. Most interesting people are busy anyway, and the intelligent ones are the ones who choose the things that keep them busy most wisely. Keeping yourself up is one of them. And Keeping At It is the cheapest and most satisfactory method.

We have already preached one sermon on the importance of clothes, but we would like to reiterate the moral, with special emphasis on the moments when nobody sees you but the family, or when nobody sees you at all. The kind of woman who gets herself up any-old-how and looks it, when there isn't company, deserves just what she gets, which might be a divorce from her husband or neglect from her friends and relatives. (We can't bring ourselves to talk about the woman who goes to bed, alone or otherwise, but especially otherwise, with her hair in curlers—except perhaps in emergencies.) [And there's no real alibi for not looking at least fresh and trim, whatever your income, what with the crisp little house dresses sold today for next to nothing, and all the other bargains.

The beauty problem may present more difficulties, but it is obvious that it can be solved, since the staggering statistics about the sale of cosmetics prove that there is no salary so small that the earner can't spend some of it on these aids to improving on Nature. If you don't do it, too, you are making a sad mistake, unless you are barely out of your teens. The only older women we have ever seen who boasted that they never used any kind of face cream got no contradictions from anybody. Just one look at them proved that they were truthful.

With a little planning and system, such Spartan abstinence is usually unnecessary even when the financial situation is acute. If these periods are prolonged, you can learn to wash your own hair, manicure your own nails, and give yourself a facial, which reduces the time and money spent in beauty shops considerably, but shouldn't eliminate them altogether (unless you're shipwrecked or exploring the African jungle, and even in these emergencies, we hope you'd manage a few beauty preparations somehow). Fortunately, we all have our good points, which take most of the care of themselves, as well as our bad points, which require constant attention. It is seldom necessary to apply everything from hair tonic to foot ease simultaneously, skipping no points between. And such universal needs as toothpastes and emollients can be purchased in the less expensive drug stores and in discount stores, as well as in beauty salons. Moreover, while the expensive ones may have a more elegant fragrance, they do not always do the work more efficiently than the less costly varieties—though here you had better check before you choose. (Incidentally, you can get a good makeshift facial by slathering cream on your face after a shampoo and before you get under the dryer, and letting it drip—and this is only one of a dozen tricks the persistent economizer can work out for herself.)

The point is to plan your spending so that you can have the things you really need for good grooming and to plan your time so that you can apply them. A well-groomed woman seldom feels completely licked, and she never looks it. Those low moments come when your hair straggles down in the nape of your neck and your hands look like a washwoman's.

A second major extravagance is to let financial pressure turn you into too good a businesswoman in matters pertaining to your personal and domestic life. Be as hard-boiled as you please during business hours, but don't start checking up grimly on the last two potatoes in the kitchen cupboard or deducting from the maid's salary when she breaks a plate. (If you can have a maid, you can afford the plate better than she can.) A man may be pretty much impressed the first time you tell him about how you didn't let the dressmaker overcharge you and how you made the cleaner come across. He may even think you're a good manager the first six times, but by the seventh, he just thinks you're difficult. (A woman knows you're stingy the third time.) A hairline separates sensible economy from the first suspicion of closeness, one of the most unlovely qualities known to humankind.

If you were born with this unfortunate trait, you'll be wise to concentrate on curing it, taking heroic measures if necessary. But above all, don't let it get to be an acquired habit. Like the Demon Rum, it will lead to no good, once it gets too firm a hold on you. You may call it by the polite term of business efficiency, but that won't change the effect it gives or fool anybody but you. Besides, even business efficiency is desirable only when it's under control. And, after all, we're not sure that it might not be better to spend your last five years in the poor house than the preceding forty-five years in the peculiar misery produced by miserliness.

Incidentally, we have often noticed that stinginess does not always save money. Mrs. Jones, who insists on getting her money's worth out of the servants, is usually the one who changes servants every two or three months, paying exorbitant temporary wages in the periods of transition; while Mrs. Smith, next door, keeps her not-too-efficient Bridget ten or fifteen years, getting all sorts of odd jobs done for love, in addition to those that are done for money, and having a very pleasant and comfortable time. Generosity has a curious way of paying back with interest.

Still another extravagance, and an obvious one, is letting your house run down any more than is necessary. It takes a lot of minor repairs to total up to the cost of the major ones that result from a few years of neglect. And we mean more than papering, painting, and not letting the roof leak. Cleverly built-in shelves, strips of mirror at the window sides, a lovely lighting fixture picked up at an auction—there are a hundred inexpensive ways to keep your house from seeming dated, and the result is not merely more fun to live in, it may also mean a better price if you want to sell or rent it.

The same principle applies to all the furnishings. You can postpone wholesale decoration for a long time by having chairs and sofas repaired at the first sign of sagging and having the table or bed fixed before it breaks down completely. Don't wait to get new slipcovers till the old ones are so shabby that you hate the pieces underneath, and don't postpone replacing broken dishes till that pattern is discontinued and you have to buy a whole new set. The lady who keeps up her linen closet and glass cupboard is a much better economist than the one who is so thrifty that she can't bear to buy anything till she is forced to by not having enough to go around.

And, of course, no woman can afford to neglect to keep up her husband's morale, or that of whatever member of her family pays for the roast and the rye. Probably the most important jobs held down during the recent financial unpleasantness were those of wives who wouldn't let their husbands feel inferior, and probably a good share of the tragedies were due to wives who didn't grasp this point. Even now that everything is Better, the idea is the same. Bucking up the person with whom you live, and doing it efficiently but without his noticing it, is what makes anybody a good wife, daughter, or what-are-you. (It is an embarrassing fact that the last are so often especially good at it.) Doing the opposite is not only hard on the man in the case, but it usually proves to be a boomerang. A husband may not be able to buy you a new silver fox, but we should think he would have to be pretty broke if he couldn't afford to take the handsome stenographer at the office out for cocktails the day after your fourth successive scene.

It all sums up to the fact that economy should be as nearly invisible as possible. This doesn't mean pretense, any more than the fact that you don't hang the soiled dish towels in the drawing room means that you haven't got any. The thing you can't afford is letting economy stand out like an ugly patch on a well-ordered life, drawing everyone's eyes away from the attractive features. This seems to us so unnecessary that it is a little stupid.

ARE YOU THRIFTY OR STINGY?

We hope no reader will be offended by being asked to serve as a Case in this chapter, since it is our embarrassed opinion that what really matters is not whether Mrs. C. or Miss X. is stingy, but whether you occasionally slip into over-economizing. If you find that you can give the correct answer of Yes or No, as the case may be, to ten of the questions that follow, you needn't be worried, but if your honest answer is wrong for a larger proportion, our advice is to watch your step.

1. Do you take friends whom you don't care about impressing to a cheap restaurant, and smart friends to an expensive one? (Think hard.)

2. At a party, do you talk loudly about ordering a taxi—and then wait to see if any of your friends with cars will offer to jitney you home?

3. When getting on a train with a friend who has a paper, do you buy a second one?

4. Do you walk instead of taking a taxi when the sidewalks are wet and you have no rubbers, or when a friend is waiting and you are late for your appointment?

5. Do you keep putting on your old dresses, and saving the new one for a more important occasion?

6. Do you forget to tip the porter on a daytime trip when he hasn't had occasion to give you any service?

7. When you are in a taxi with a lot of women, are you a past master at the art of fumbling?

8. Do you hang on to old dresses that you don't wear, but think you might have made over some time, instead of sending them to the Salvation Army or some other charity?

9. Do you check your restaurant bill before paying it?

10. Do you wear a nightgown or a slip just once more, even though it's a shade soiled, before putting it into the clothes hamper?

11. Do you buy Christmas presents that will do for relatives to whom giving is a duty, instead of trying to think of something they would really like?

12. Do you buy second-rate liquor, thinking you can doctor up the taste with the other ingredients in the cocktails?

13. Do you painstakingly untie the string on packages?

14. Do you salve your conscience after the extravagance of buying a hat you didn't need by lunching in a drug store on tea and a cheap sandwich?

15. Do you forget to pay for telephone calls in other people's houses?

(You'll find the answers below.)

THIS WILL TELL YOU THE WORST

1. Yes. (The unstylish ones are often more at home in a not-too-smart restaurant and might think you were showing off if you took them to a smart one, especially if you can't afford to. It's better to choose one where the guests won't feel dowdy—but where the food is good.)

2. No. (The fact that a friend has a car doesn't mean that it is convenient for her to drive all over town. This is an all-too-common form of sponging. People who can't get themselves to and from parties ought to stay home unless they are certain that someone really wants to take them.)

3. Yes. (What you save by not buying a newspaper doesn't begin to pay for the irritation most people feel at having to share one. And why should they?)

4. No. (Getting your shoes wet is a definite extravagance—they seldom look quite the same again. And keeping other people waiting is selfish.)

5. No. (If you do this at all, you are pretty sure to do it too often, and one fine day you find that the new dress isn't so new or so smart and that you've had scarcely any wear out of it.)

6. No. (A porter's pay presupposes tips and he's entitled to them.)

7. No. (This shouldn't need explaining.)

8. No. (You probably won't have them made over and, anyway, someone who needs them more might be getting a lot of wear and pleasure out of them.)

9. Yes. (This isn't stinginess. Everyone makes mistakes sometimes, but you needn't pay for other people's.)

10. No. (Fastidiousness is a quality you can't afford to be without.)

11. No. (If you don't see why for yourself, you *are* stingy.)

12. No. (If you did, while you might deserve the headache the next morning, your guests wouldn't, and we hope they wouldn't come again.)

13. Yes. (This is a harmless economy, and it often comes in handy.)

14. No. (What you save by not eating more lunch doesn't make up for the hat, and you need more nourishment after a shopping bout and are likely to make your family do the paying up by being cross that evening.)

15. No. (Answering this incorrectly should count as two mistakes!)

CHAPTER SIX

YOU HAVE TO EAT

THERE ARE a lot of things that you can just toss out of your life like so much dead wood, when you come to a barren stretch, but food isn't one of them. Three times a day you've got to eat—or, at any rate, you ought to eat, all people with fancy food schedules to the contrary. There may be those who can get along on peanuts and dates eaten at odd hours, but it is our inexpert opinion that they are queer ducks who like what it does to their ego more than they dislike what it does to their health. Anyway, we are all for three square meals a day, and there are few things from which we, and most of the people we know, get more fun.

Not so long ago, too much enthusiasm about food was looked down on. Sophisticated but maidless matrons went in for meetings instead of menus, and you heard a lot of elegantly snooty talk about the lowly kitchen minded. (We hate to think what came out of their kitchens, and the thought of their husbands sets us to brooding.) Now, however, food has become highbrow, the best people are gourmets, and it has dawned upon the majority of intelligent women that their minds should be able to take in the kitchen, along with a lot of other things.

Too much fuss is made over the drudgery of getting three meals a day—a fairly simple process that has been mastered by all sorts of brains the world over for a good many years. We aren't suggesting that you serve the meals of peasant Russia (though you might get an idea from them), or that, if you're maidless, getting meals won't take time. But you can plan them so that they won't take too *much* time, and if you put a little imagination into them, getting them shouldn't be dull. Creating anything, from a symphony to a soufflé, interests anyone with a spark inside.

One of the pleasantest things in life is having a reputation as an outstanding person, and whether you do your standing out as a prima donna or a cook makes less difference in your personal satisfaction than you may think. If you've got to be the cook anyway, it's a little short of stupid to stew because you can't be the prima donna.

It is therefore our hard-boiled advice, if you come to a stretch when you have to get all the meals and get them as inexpensively as possible besides, to make this little chore your hobby and do it with an air. Nothing can be duller (both in the getting and in the eating) than uninteresting food on a drab table. But there is such a vogue for simple, yet interesting, food today that corned-beef hash and coleslaw, served with chic, can seem like something copied from the smartest house. (It may be just that, in fact.) It canalso, served unattractively, seem like pretty poor pickings.

The trick is to have a little real knowledge about food and service, to put imagination into your meals, and to organize the time you spend on them. If you haven't got the first, you can get it by reading the smartest of the magazines that go into hostess's problems, perusing a few of the best cookbooks (you can do this at the public library—a place few women use enough), and spending fifteen minutes every time you go shopping in the linen, china, and glass departments of the stores you visit. This doesn't mean that you need buy everything you see, or even anything, but it ought to give you some ideas that you can carry out for next to nothing.

One of the gayest tables we have ever seen had black-and-tan checked linen (perhaps near-linen would be more exact), yellow pottery, amber glassware, yellow marigolds in a black bowl, and salad in a wooden bowl. The pottery, glass, and wooden bowl came out of a discount store, and the marigolds came out of the garden. We have also seen an engaging red, white, and blue table, with blue-and-white striped Basque linen, blue china, red glass, and a white bowl holding red, white, and blue garden flowers.

You couldn't have a smarter background for dinner than a gray or a salmony-pink damask cloth, acquired by dipping an old white one in Tintex and used with the white china that is now so incredibly inexpensive. And green and white makes an enchanting table that can be worked out for a song, with white candles for accents and leaves in a white bowl, making flowers unnecessary.

These are minor extravagances, just a bit of bubbly on your budget, and a type of thing you'd better go in for. You'll need them as a stimulus to keep up your enthusiasm seven days a week, which isn't easy, but can be done, to your own satisfaction and the envy of your friends.

One obvious bit of advice is to go to market, but we don't mean the market just around the corner. We mean an outdoor market, or a foreign one, or an odd shop in which you might make discoveries. Don't be too set about the shopping list you take with you; browse around. Italian markets have all sorts of unusual salad greens and unfamiliar vegetables. The cheapest one may be the best, because it's at the height of its season. There are exciting things to be found in Spanish grocery stores, and Swedish delicatessens, and Mexican shops, and Chinese sections, and stores that carry food to suit the tastes of Russians and Hungarians and Armenians and a dozen other nationalities. If there are any—or all—of these in your town or city, do a little investigating, and look for herbs, and queer cheeses, and unusual sauces. If you don't know what they are or what to do with them, don't buy them then; make a note and read up on them and pick them up next time, if you think you'd like them. And it's a good idea to talk to friendly foreign shopkeepers—you may get a recipe for a buffet supper dish that will make you famous.

You'll have to work out your own housekeeping system to suit your own circumstances, but be sure you have a system. Without it, you'll find yourself spending all sorts of odd and unnecessary hours going domestic. Some women do everything up with a bang right after breakfast, and by everything, they mean all but the last-minute gestures for luncheon and dinner. (With a little planning, there need be very few of these.) This system usually means shopping the afternoon before, or spending the last half of a couple of mornings a week on a marketing orgy. Whatever you do, don't forget that one of the advantages of not having a maid is that meals can be movable and elastic. If your husband wants to work in the garden, or your son wants to stop at the club for a game of squash, there's nothing against it—unless, of course, you are one of those women who use this as an excuse for complaining about how you're a slave in the kitchen all day, and they don't even care enough to come home on time to meals. (You might try being a slave in the office some summer day; and perhaps you can remember that you weren't so enthusiastic even about being a slave in school.) But the leniency ought to apply to you too. It's a good idea to keep a well-stocked emergency shelf of things in tins that can be whipped into a meal in a few moments. There are plenty of them, these days, and some of them are marvellous, and—if you watch for sales—not too expensive. With this shelf behind you, you can put on your hat without a qualm when someone suggests a game of bridge or a drive into the country.

Without going into menus, may we murmur at this point that the fact that you can't buy the most expensive meats or the most elegant trimmings for your meals is not a world tragedy? Radishes, or crisped raw carrot fingers or the black Greek olives that cost so little are as popular as more expensive tidbits; and such things as steaks and roasts are so well prepared in the best restaurants that you might seem to turn up your nose at them for home cooking—and get away with it too. There are innumerable things to try instead, of course, some of them even more delicious and lots of them just as good.

Try, for instance, sausages surrounded by Yorkshire pudding and baked in a pan. Or substitute chops for the sausages; you can make one chop do for each person, helped out by the pudding. Or serve boiled tongue with a very special sauce, like a Russian mustard sauce with sherry in it, or horseradish sauce. (Learning to make sauces will get you a reputation as a cook in no time—so few have a varied and sophisticated sauce repertoire; though a sauce can be the touch that gives chic to a meal.) Or try one of the endless varieties of risottos, which nearly everybody likes, with the rice reducing the amount of meat you need; or a curry made from one of the less expensive cuts of lamb or veal. With this, of course, you must have a heaping dish of rice and plenty of condiments—such as chopped onions, slivered peanuts, chopped eggs (the whites and yolks separate), chopped green peppers, grated coconut, French-fried onion rings, and chutney. You don't need all of these, but have several, and very little else. A green salad and light dessert and coffee make a smarter meal with curry than a lot of fancy food. And we know of one hostess famous for her curry dinners who always starts them with a very thin purée of leeks, served in a lovely old tureen. (She uses the tureen for flowers when it isn't used for soup.)

Almost any man will brighten up under a superlative beef stew, flavored perhaps with a little Madeira. And a kidney stew, made with beef kidneys, mushrooms, cream, and a dash of sherry just before serving is something to grow lyrical about. There are also such economies as beef-steak rolls, made from the inexpensive top or bottom round of beef, cut in very thin slices, and spread with stuffing like that used for roast chicken before being rolled up. These are extra good when served with mushroom sauce, which is a versatile sauce and cheap when mushrooms are in season. Try it over egg timbales, or a macaroni mold or spinach ring, as a luncheon dish at your next party.

And don't forget those Spanish and Mexican dishes that are meals in themselves and favorites with so many people. These will win you a reputation as a marvellous cook even quicker than the repertoire of sauces, and this reputation, though the most easily acquired distinction we know of, is well worth having. Most people are more impressed by a sophisticated knowledge of food and cooking than by an erudite discourse on political economy, and practically everybody is more interested. One specialty will start the reputation, and two or three will cinch it, and after that, guests will flock to your house like homing pigeons, given half a chance.

It is particularly impressive, of course, if you can saddle your husband with the reputation, as men cooks are invariably looked upon with awe. If he has the faintest hint of a flair for cooking, fan it like a dying flame; it may prove to be a tremendous asset in entertaining. If he really likes it, you are made as a hostess. You can surround his humblest efforts with pomp and ceremony that will give any party a grand air—and his efforts probably won't be humble long anyway. Men who can cook take their talent pretty seriously, and you will soon find your kitchen shelves littered with strange herbs, queer vinegars, and a tempting assortment of wines suitable for cooking. The oddest requests along this line should be encouraged like the first signs of talent in a budding Shirley Temple; there's no telling how profitable the results may be.

This brings us to the matter of entertaining, which is something you shouldn't give up unless the condition of your bank account is really alarming. You don't need to entertain expensively. It doesn't even need to be a lot of work. (If giving a party seems to you a terrific undertaking, try staying home the night before and going to bed early with a good book.) But entertaining is important. Both the parties you give and the parties you go to (and you can't expect to go to them unless you give them) are stimulating and good for making and keeping friends and bolstering your morale. They are another of the extravagances that pay, and every budget should be planned to cover them.

Being embarrassed by having to entertain simply is a silly form of snobbery, in these days when simple meals are smarter than fancy ones anyway, and an amusing party is far more of an achievement than an elaborate one. It's not a matter of what it costs; it's a matter of knowing how and being willing to take the trouble.

It needn't even be much trouble. Real hospitality and carefully combined guests are the most important parts of any party. You can't fake the first by paying for it, and the second doesn't cost a cent more than a bad assortment.

One of the first rules is not to attempt more than you can manage. You ought to be able to manage *something*, no matter where or how you live. The modern generation, pricked by necessity, has invented all sorts of ways of entertaining on a shoestring, most of them far less stodgy than the nine-course dinners and lobster-salad-and-ice-cream receptions of our parents' time. They are the ones you will find living in a gardener's cottage and inviting twenty friends to a Sunday lunch of glorified baked ham and superlative potato salad, with coffee and the cherries that formed the centerpiece for dessert. Or perhaps they live in a bandbox of a house on the outskirts of a suburb, and invite you to a skating party, taking you to the pond in a borrowed painter's truck and feeding you afterward on cheese and hamburger and beer and coffee. Or it may be that they have an apartment in town, in a not very smart section, and the party is a late supper after the movies, with the makings of drinks and sandwiches laid out on the table—a variety of breads and crackers; bowls of such spreads as Roquefort cheese with chopped celery and mayonnaise, or chopped ham and pickle; plates of liverwurst and other cold meats; a jar of special mustard; several cheeses; and bottles of beer and ginger ale and scotch and rye and soda. At this party, the guests do all the work and like it.

If these ideas don't fit you—what about Sunday morning brunch, with as many guests as you can fit into your dining room—or living room, or, if you live in the country and it's summer, your porch? Almost everyone likes a Sunday with brunch, now that the large Sunday dinner, that used to be served in the middle of the day and reduce us all to a state of stuffed drowsiness, is going out as completely as the buggy. The budgeting hostess likes it particularly, because, at the hour when brunch is served—eleven, perhaps, or even twelve (you can go to church in the afternoon or evening, that Sunday)—her guests don't want alcoholic drinks, or shouldn't have them, if they do. All that she needs to provide in the way of liquid refreshments is fruit juice, preferably in tall glass pitchers and very cold, and lots of hot coffee. Orange juice and grapefruit juice are general favorites and enough, but if the party is large, she might have a row of pitchers, each with a different fruit juice—orange, grapefruit, pineapple, apricot, prune, and what-have-you. She might, of course, add such things as huge bowls of berries or cut-up peaches or cantaloupe, but it isn't necessary. There should, however, be a variety of toast and hot muffins (popovers are invariably popular, and blueberry muffins are sure to make a sensation); a selection of marmalade, honey and jams; and at least two hot dishes to choose from. Scotch oatmeal with brown sugar and cream always seems to surprise people pleasantly and costs very little, and almost all men like really good codfish balls, while scrambled eggs with sausages are surefire, if not startling, and heaping plates of pancakes with maple syrup appeal to even the dieters.

At the risk of being monotonous, may we say that the setting can do a lot for or against the party, and that it isn't a matter of what it costs? A long table set in a sunny window, or on a terrace with a view, or out under an apple tree, can have the simplest china and linen and look enchanting. You might, for instance, use the brown Mexican ware that is so cheap, and a copper bowl with zinnias to match the orange juice, and those deep brown covered casseroles or bean pots for the hot dishes. You'll find the latter endlessly useful at buffet suppers.

We needn't tell you that buffet suppers are a triumphant solution of the no-maid-and-little-money party. They are, in fact, so successful that plenty of people with several maids and lots of money go in for them. One of the chief advantages is that everything can be got ready—or very nearly ready—well in advance, which is something a maidless hostess should aim for. A really skillful one does this so thoroughly that an hour or so before the guests arrive she is peacefully stretched out in a tub of fragrant warm water, relaxing, and *not* counting the napkins mentally.

The best buffet suppers are planned so that everyone can sit down in a group, with a small table at hand to avoid the necessity of balancing plate, cup, glass, and fork like a juggler. This is almost as important as the food, which can be as simple as you like, so long as it's good. Begin with a soup if you want to—though you don't need to—but if you do, make it a very special soup, like chicken curry soup (made from chicken consommé, the juice of chopped onion and apple, cream, and curry powder), or a black bean soup with lemon. Have two hot dishes, a salad, rolls, a light dessert, and coffee, and plan them all with an eye to cheapness and without embarrassment.

You might, for instance, choose from among any of the following not-too-costly entrées: a casserole of diced ham and hard-boiled eggs in cream sauce; corned-beef hash; curried eggs; corn pudding; halibut mousse with horseradish sauce; salmon mold with tartar sauce; macaroni mold with mushroom sauce; macaroni with Italian sauce (with tomatoes, ham, tongue, mushrooms, Parmesan cheese, and a hint of garlic); baked beans; creamed mushrooms; crabflakes and hard-boiled eggs in a sherry-flavored cream sauce; succotash; and a very special stew with tiny white onions, potato balls, and baby carrots. As for the salad, there is nothing so smart or inexpensive as a mixed-green salad bowl with lettuce, chicory, escarole, watercress, celery, radishes, shredded cabbage, diced carrots, tomatoes, and cucumbers—any or all of them, tossed in an Epicurean French dressing. The cost is amazingly little and the most critical gourmet will be impressed if the dressing is what it should be.

Before you plan your party—buffet or otherwise—it's a good idea to take stock of your assets. If you have a fireplace, plan the party around that. This means that small groups will be better than large ones, and in this case, you might follow one hostess's bright brain wave and have two on successive nights, thereby using the same decorations and getting the house into party order only once. Another smart hostess, who had no dining room, but had comfortable sofas and chairs grouped around a big fireplace, bought herself two nests of small tables and used these instead of one large one. When dinner was served, a small table was put in front of each guest, set as though for a formal dinner, and the meal was served with all the elegance of dinner in a baronial hall.

A fireplace is a special asset to the woman who lives alone. What she can accomplish with a becoming hostess gown and a well-planned dinner served on a small table in the firelight—and a masculine guest—is something she ought to be able to figure out without any help from us.

A spot in your garden or terrace, if you have one, is another thing to use effectively, as you can with a little planning. All women love to eat outdoors (it seems to appeal to something in their romantic natures) and most men can be persuaded to and kept sufficiently amused so that they forget the curious masculine prejudice against meals served anywhere except at the dining room table.

Still another thing to feature is a silver tea set. If you have an old and lovely one, and little else so elegant, have more tea parties and fewer other forms of entertainment, and learn to pour tea charmingly. A tea party can have a very special atmosphere, given a gracious hostess, and the cost of this is next to nothing. Thin slices of bread and butter, or cinnamon toast, and the smallest, simplest cakes are far smarter than a lot of fancy food. (We won't insult you by even mentioning fancy salads or ice cream served in the afternoon.) Or if you have a piano and a musician in your family, have supper parties with singing afterward, in a room lighted with lots of candles.

Bridge is, of course, the simplest solution to the entertaining problem, since it demands nothing but two packs of cards, a table, and a tray afterward with something like beer or highballs or tall glasses of fruit juice and a cheese board with well-selected cheeses and crackers. The choice of cheeses is, incidentally, a telltale detail—few things in the food line show more sophisticated knowledge of food, or the opposite. (Imported Roquefort, Camembert, Cheddar, and Bel Paese are all safe choices.) If you don't want to play bridge—and there is less and less of the feeling that it is the only parlor game—you can still serve refreshments after bingo played for pennies or the murder game or whatever is your own idea of sports in the living room.

There are times, however, when nothing but a dinner party will do, but even this needn't be a poser, though it does involve more work and slightly more expense. These things can be reduced to a minimum if you know how, but it does take planning and ingenuity. A good way to begin is to substitute wines for cocktails, but you must know your wines. A lot of enterprising economizers are going into the matter thoroughly these days and having a lot of fun discovering good wines at small prices. In New York, many of the Italian wine shops up and down Second Avenue have Italian wines that are excellent and cost surprisingly little. There are numerous other bargains too—but it's wise to consult a man who knows the good ones from the poor ones before you buy. Some one of your friends is pretty sure to be a wine fancier, and he'll like nothing better than to tell you all about it. Good wines not only add éclat to any dinner party; they also add a lot of appreciation, for there's no denying that cocktails dull one's discrimination about food, though they may sharpen the appetite with which it's eaten. And you can get a good wine for less money than you pay for a mediocre cocktail.

Another good idea is to work up one perfect menu till you can turn it out with practically no effort. This is something to be considered by both a maid-less hostess and one with an inexperienced maid or two. It means a few rehearsals, but if it's a really good menu, nobody will mind and you will have more confidence and less flurry the night of the party. You can use it again and again, on different guests, with success and practically no trouble.

All of this sums up to the fact that parties belong on every budget and that what they cost is up to you. At the best parties, the chief ingredients are originality (which doesn't mean whimsy or—heaven forbid—paper favors) and a lot of enthusiasm.

CASES

Case XIX: Mr. L. and Mr. E.—Mr. L. and Mr. E. are two smart young men-about-town who share an apartment and have built up a reputation for their "little dinners" that might be a lesson to the rest of us. Their theory is to do everything possible (which they manage to make practically everything) sometime before the guests arrive, so that there are no evidences of hard manual labor on their part, and also so that they can have an elegant time at their own parties. The menus vary only slightly, the main dish always being of the casserole type—a system that not only simplifies the planning, but keeps the equipment down to a minimum.

They start off with cocktails and a few very small, simple, appetizing sandwiches, served in the living room, of course. Dinner begins with a thin soup with the addition of lemon or chives, and proceeds to a large casserole, a very mixed green salad (always with some unexpected green included), and crusty rolls. A small dessert and extra-black coffee complete the menu.

Mr. L. is responsible for the main dishes and has invented several that have given him a reputation as an amateur chef that is almost embarrassing. One is a fish dish with sole and white grapes, the fame of which has spread until this dish is now served in various smart New York restaurants. Another, also with sole, includes onions, tomatoes, and sour cream. And a third is a duck pie. All in all, an invitation to one of Mr. L.'s and Mr. E.'s little dinners is something to wangle for.

Case XX: Mrs. K.—Mrs. K. is an ambitious divorcée with plenty of friends and very little money. She has, however, a large supply of ingenuity and she decided recently that, poor or not, it was high time she caught up with her social obligations.

These, listed on paper, proved to be somewhat staggering, but Mrs. K. wasn't staggered long. She made up her mind to have a double party, inviting those she owed a little for cocktails and those she owed a lot to stay on afterward, thereby doing everything up with one fell swoop and saving herself both trouble and expense.

Mrs. K. cleared most of the furniture out of the living room and sent invitations right and left. The first event, being a cocktail party, wasn't cheap, but it cleared up a lot of social debts at a fairly low cost. She kept expenses down as much as possible by serving gin drinks, and none with whiskey, and by making the tidbits of such things as peanut butter mixed with chili sauce and spread on rounds of toast; smoked beef rolled around cottage cheese flavored with horseradish; cheese popcorn; and shreds of raw carrots crisped in iced saltwater.

The second event was a buffet supper, with only hamburgers (the best in town), bowls of very special homemade potato salad, and coffee. One of the guests played an accordian for dancing, alternating with the radio, and a good time was had by all far into the night.

Case XXI: Mrs. V.—Mrs. V. is a bride who came to a small city where she had few acquaintances and who felt that it was important to establish a position for her husband and herself, in spite of an infinitesimal salary. She decided to concentrate on Tea, and she did it with such success that no one has noticed yet that that is her only way of entertaining.

Mrs. V. has one advantage in her wedding silver tea set, which gives an unquestionable air. She prepares the tray every morning, as soon as she has done the breakfast dishes and cleaned up the apartment, exactly as though she expected guests for tea that afternoon. Sugar is put in the sugar bowl, tea in the teapot, and spoons and tea napkins are laid out in readiness. Only the actual food is missing, and Mrs. V. always has something planned. It may be small tea biscuits and a pot of special strawberry jam (the biscuits are served for dinner if nobody comes), or a pecan coffee cake that she can use next morning for breakfast. It may be crisp crackers sprinkled with grated cheese that she can pop into the oven either at teatime or with the salad at dinner. Or it may be cookies or little cakes that are equally good served with tea or dessert.

When callers first came to see the bride, out came the tray, as though it were a daily rite. So expected did it seem to be that people soon took it for granted that she always did have tea, and as acquaintances grew into friends, dropping in on Mrs. V. at teatime became a common occurrence, this being a pleasant way to end any hectic— or dullish—afternoon. Mrs. V.'s living room seems to have a special air at tea-time. She has made a specialty of the things she serves with tea, which include several varieties of unusual and particularly good breads, cut thin and spread with butter. She makes elegant cinnamon toast, and has scoured the town for such things as cinnamon buns and other pastries, and she has a half dozen varieties of small cakes and cookies, all made at a very small cost, which she keeps on hand. But more than this, she has learned to make the serving a ceremony that has a hint of elegance.

Mrs. V.'s circle of friends has grown with surprising rapidity, and the V.'s are now often invited out. Mr. V. is finding this a distinct advantage in his business, and Mrs. V. enjoys returning her obligations by giving Sunday-afternoon tea parties, with husbands included.

Case XXII: Mrs. Z.—Mrs. Z. is a suburban wife who has always had a maid and has never had a flair for cooking. Her particular problem has long been Sunday-night suppers, Mr. Z. not being one who is satisfied with a snack out of the icebox. He seems to feel, moreover, that Sunday night should be a pleasant climax to a weekend holiday.

This attitude put Mrs. Z., who aims to please, on the spot—until she had the bright idea of hornswoggling Mr. Z. into being the chef. Having noted that if a man cooked at all, he did it with more than the solemnity which he applied to his business, she began by telling him all about the smart New York men who went in for cooking. Before she had finished, Mr. Z. was led to believe that practically any man worth anything could toss off a rarebit or an omelet and he wondered if he couldn't too, if he tried. Soon after this, she tried a little flattery as to Mr. Z.'s really remarkable knowledge of food—a subject on which the best of us like to be flattered. And the next Sunday evening, she concluded her triumphant campaign by leaving him for a moment (which grew into ten) with a chafing dish full of crabflake Newburg that required only stirring and a dash from the nearby bottle of sherry.

Mrs. Z. was lavish in her praise of the masterly way in which Mr. Z. rose to the emergency, and he thought that he hadn't done so badly himself. The Newburg was undeniably delicious. It was easy after this to work him into two or three specialties, most of which are painstakingly prepared by the maid before she leaves for town, but which Mr. Z. completes to the intense admiration of the friends whom he invites in with that in mind. As the friends do most of the serving, the rest of the meal is left ready in the icebox, and Mrs. Z. leaves the dishes for the maid to do on Monday morning, Sunday nights have ceased to be a very difficult problem.

CHAPTER SEVEN

DO IT ANYWAY

THE NONE-TOO-SPARTAN title of this chapter does not mean, as you might suppose: Do it whether you can pay for it or not; it does mean: Use your ingenuity and figure out a way by which you can pay for it. This is not nearly so impossible as it seems at first glance. It is, in fact, the usual formula for Getting On In The World.

It's very easy to settle back and say you can't afford whatever it is that's on your mind, thereby giving yourself an excuse for being thoroughly miserable. But however much you may enjoy this state, it's pretty tiresome to everybody else and never gets you anywhere. You'll come out much better in the end if you study ways and means, and throw in a little imagination.

Plenty of people have done this with enviable results. Even women tied down by large families and small incomes. In such a predicament, you might, for instance, if your talents run to bridge playing, teach bridge. Most towns and cities are full of would-be players who would pay a sympathetic teacher for instructions, especially if they didn't have to pay too much. Or you might use some other talent as a basis for turning teacher. We know of one woman who was extra-good at making her own clothes and who let her friends and neighbors bring in their patterns and materials, for a slight charge, while she helped them cut and fit. The great advantage of this system is that you usually have fun along with the work, as everybody likes to do the things she does well.

The chief thing *not* to do is to stew because you can't go out into the world and make money. You don't have to go out into the world. There are dozens of things you can do in a bandbox of an apartment or on a farm forty miles from town. You can write or paint or design, for instance, or you might type (though perhaps not on the farm) or make pickles or knit or compose music. We know of one woman who turned her enclosed porch into a shop and sold dresses. She lived in a suburb and was smart enough to sell only the shirtwaist type, really well-cut and made in a variety of fabrics from soft cashmeres to washable silks, with a few (very few) more formal ones thrown in, and her clothes were so exactly right for the life in that community that she built up a really good business. Another woman sold lovely handmade lingerie and négligées, carefully selected from good wholesalers, using the guest room as a salesroom. She kept the lingerie in the deep drawers of a beautiful old ancestral highboy and the négligées in a closet painted pink and trimmed with ruffled organdy shelf edging, and she had next to no overhead and could charge a little less than the lingerie cost in most shops. You'd be surprised at her Christmas business. A knitting shop in your living room (if you're a talented knitter), with wools and tweeds by the yard to match; a lending library with books which you yourself deliver in the family car; a garden with some speciality like delphinium (if you are one of those who can make things grow a little better than the next person)—these are only a few of the ways to get what you want. You'll probably get it quicker if you think up your own way. The point is to get it.

One young woman who loved to be doing things and whose husband's salary couldn't be stretched to cover classes and clubs, got what *she* wanted by forming the classes and having them in her own living room, thereby getting her class membership free. She started with tap dancing and French the first year and has been through a variety of courses since, having an elegant time.

We have long passed the time when there was any social stigma attached to earning as much money as you can, though there are still some methods to be avoided. In general, however, prestige goes along with a good business, and plenty of women go straight from work to the most exclusive parties. We are not denying that you may have an old-fashioned parent, or even a husband, who feels that your labors cast a slur on his earning capacity, but if he can't or won't come across with the things you want, we advise you to go ahead anyway for a time at least. The chances are that his sputtering will turn into pride if you do a good job.

And don't think that you can't Get Around on very little money (and a lot of enterprise). There are few if any cities that don't have inexpensive restaurants (especially the foreign ones) with food good enough so that you can look on them as discoveries and not as drab necessities. And it's no secret that matinées are less expensive than evening shows. Making a point to attend matinées allows you to stay current on the latest films and plays, an important part of the culture, without overspending. They also allow you to keep your evenings free for relaxing or other activities. If you don't like these ideas, think up your own. Anything from a Yogi gathering to a picnic can be interesting if you have an open mind.

We've already said that you ought to give parties, or at least a party now and then, and we don't want to be told that parties cost money. We know that already, but we also know that the best parties are not the ones that cost the *most* money. There is a young man in New York, for instance, who went around with plutocrats and who had the commendable desire (not shared by all current young men) of wanting to return courtesies, but who had an infinitesimal income. He therefore gave a boat party in the Sound, hiring not an elegant boat that he couldn't afford, but the cheapest tub he could find, which was much more of a novelty to his rich friends. Its lack of elegance broke down their reserve, if any, to the point where they sang lustily in the moonlight, after the picnic supper and along with the highballs.

Another young man took a group of his friends on a hot summer night to the terrace on the eighty-sixth floor of the Empire State Building, where the sunset is breathtaking and the view of the city after dark is Something.

There is live music and the breeze is just as refreshing as in the most expensive hostelries.

In New York, there are inexpensive summer-night boat trips and if you go to the top decks, you will leave most of the hoi-polloi below you and sail through one of the most spectacular harbors in the world in peace and quiet. You may have to pick your way through banana skins, babies, and beer bottles on the lower deck when you embark, but if you go on-board early, you'll never know they are there till the end of the trip. The owners don't seem to be interested in privacy. And there are outdoor cafeterias and snack stands in New York, run by the Park Commission, with food at which you shouldn't turn up your nose.

We don't know what your town offers, but we'll wager it offers something we wish we did know about.

One more thing To Do Anyway is to give presents, and especially Christmas presents. It's surprising how many people find it necessary to do their economizing right here. Sadly and nobly they tell their friends and relatives that they can't manage gifts this year and they know it's going to spoil Christmas for them. We hope it does, but we doubt it.

Your income is in a bad way if you can't give a few presents, with thought taking the place of most of the money. Some of the most engaging presents we've ever had have cost next to nothing, and some of the most expensive have been frankly Gosh Presents (meaning the kind of presents that make you say "Gosh!" when you open the package). Someone once gave us a Gumdrop Tree that she'd made from the branch of a thorn tree, stuck in a pot and silvered all over, with colored gumdrops shimmering on every thorn. It stood in the window and was the most enchanting Christmas decoration of the season. And we once had a pile of mirrored plaques to put under flower vases given us. They came from a discount store and were tied with a gay ribbon, and we're still using them with the greatest pleasure. Another ingenious giver sent all her friends who had fireplaces great bags of big cones that she'd gathered herself in the country. The bags were made of pale green argentine catstitched with silver cord and tied at the top with a huge silver bow, and everybody loved them.

If you're a good shopper, you can pick up innumerable bargains in old glass and china at secondhand stores and thrift shops. Now and then, a discount store will have some really charming china, and you can make up a flowered breakfast tray set for not much at all. Usually, you can find smart cocktail glasses, or a decorative box that you can turn into a weekend beauty box and pack with the smallest-sized packages of beauty preparations (also from a discount store). And these are merely starters, a few suggestions among the thousands of possibilities.

There are, in fact, so many possibilities that we doubt if many people get away with their hard-luck stories about how they just can't manage Christmas this year. Most listeners look polite, but know better.

CASES

Case XXIII: Mr. and Mrs. D.—When Mr. and Mrs. D. were married, twenty years ago, they were able to travel (their favorite pastime) only by saving pennies scrupulously, watching for special excursion rates, and going inexpensively and infrequently. They had a marvellous time, however, when they did go—and they continued to be travel enthusiasts later on when Mr. D. had made enough money to take them on a fancy cruise liner, engage rooms at the Ritzes, and rent an automobile whenever it was a convenience.

After several of these elegant tours, the Depression arrived—just in time to spoil their newest plan for a really extensive trip. Mr. D. had read reams of preparatory literature, they had picked out the romantic spots they particularly wanted to see, and he thought he had figured out a way to leave his business safely. But suddenly there was very little business to leave. They decided reluctantly that the grand tour would have to wait for another year.

It waited for several years. Even then, though things were looking up, they were not looking as high as the plans for the journey. This kept being shoved further and further into the future, until one day Mrs. D. confronted Mr. D. with a firm look in her eye.

"Look here," she said. "I'm not a hundred and I'm not decrepit. I'm still in my forties, in fact, and going strong—and so are you. I don't have to travel on the *Queen Mary* or the *Normandie*, nice as they are. I can still get around enough to go on a small, cheap ship, or even a freighter, if that's all we can pay for. I don't have to have the best cabin or a private bath, any more than I did when we first went places. I can get into a bus just as well as a private automobile, and I can eat in a cheap café as well as the most expensive restaurants. We had fun doing all these things once, and I don't see why we can't now. We could just about afford them. Let's take the trip."

Mr. D., who had long ago learned the uselessness of combatting Mrs. D. in this particular mood and who wanted to go anyway, eventually agreed. They were gone two months and they discovered that they were perfectly comfortable in a cheap cabin, that they still had enough charm and good humor to win them the friendship of the nicest of their fellow travellers, that in some less-visited coun-  tries their third-class accommodations turned out to be the same as the first, and that in the places where there was a great difference, the difference could usually be made into an adventure.

They had an even better time than on their previous trips and got back to find that business had picked up enough so that Mr. D. had made more money while he was away than in any two months for several years.

Case XXIV: Mr. and Mrs. I.—Although Mr. and Mrs. I. are young and each has a very small salary, they have one extravagance that is an envy and puzzle to all their friends. They live far uptown in New York and their budget is carefully planned, but they manage to see all the best plays. Comedy, tragedy, and musical shows—they can tell you all about any of them and their conversation is full of dramatic enthusiasm.

How, their friends wonder, with theater tickets so high for all the successes, can they manage to do it?

They manage by laying their plans carefully. They read the dramatic criticisms religiously and, whenever a play sounds good, one of them goes next day and buys two seats in the front row of the top balcony for the first free night when they are to be had. Often, this turns out to be that very night or the next one, before the news of success has spread. Sometimes it is several weeks later and frequently on a Monday night.

They seldom waste money on the poor plays, but when, as occasionally happens, a badly reviewed play continues to run and climbs into popularity, they stop in at the places that sell tickets at cut rates, going early in the week when theater-goers are not so numerous. They sometimes have orchestra seats at top-gallery prices—and they always have fun.

Case XXV: Miss A.—Miss A. is a woman who for years felt great satisfaction in the fact that, though she started her career without training, she was successful enough to be more than comfortable with no help from her relations. She had a four-room apartment, a maid by the day, and a black caracul coat, which she thought ought to be enough for anybody. She also saw a good proportion of the best plays in town, went occasionally to the opera, lunched or dined now and then in the smartest restaurants, and took cruises on vacation.

A time came, however, when the firm with which Miss A. was employed was reorganized and a man took over her work. Because of her efficiency and the length of time she had worked there, the firm offered her another position— but at about half the former salary. Even this was as much as many women get, she realized, and she could economize quite as well as they could—but these points did not minimize the sting to Miss A.'s pride. She wouldn't mind wearing last year's dresses (until she'd found a way to make more money, which might take time, at her age), but she would very much mind having her brother-in-law and that rather snooty cousin know she wasn't making the money she used to make.

It then occurred to Miss A. that, if she was really bright, they didn't have to know it. She tramped the city till she found a one-room-and-kitchenette apartment in which the one room was large and had both atmosphere and a view. She furnished it with the best of her possessions and extremely good taste, and then spread the news that she had discovered an apartment with exactly the view she'd always wanted and that it so enchanted her that she simply *had* to have it, even though she'd be a trifle cramped for space.

Once settled, she entertained less often, but no less well, and enlarged conversationally on how busy she'd been— as, in fact, she was, since she now had a maid only occasionally and kept her own clothes in order. (When she did entertain, however, there were white calla lily—bought in a bargain basement—in a pale glass vase in the window; caviar—eked out with chopped egg—on the canapés; and crème de menthe—left from prosperous days— served with coffee.) She seldom bought a theater ticket or went to an expensive restaurant, though she managed a very few of even these extravagances. And her meals at home were miracles of nourishing economy.

Miss A.'s reward came one Sunday evening when both her brother-in-law and the snooty cousin were among her guests at a buffet supper (the only one she gave that season). She happened to mention the fact that she'd been helping a friend work out a very limited budget.

To her surprise and pleasure, everybody—including the relatives—burst into loud laughter.

"What do you, of all people, know about economy?" the cousin said.

"What indeed?" thought Miss A. triumphantly.

CHAPTER EIGHT

ALMOST BALANCING THE BUDGET

WE HAVE now come to that bad moment when we can no longer see any possible way of avoiding a few words on the unpleasant subject of budgets. The moment is bad because we suspect that the haphazard system that we gaily refer to as budgeting wouldn't be thought to rate the title by any technical budgeteer. Our only defence is that it works.

It works, that is, for us. But our firm belief is that budgeting is as personal a matter as love, and that it's one of the things you have to work out for yourself, with a little help collected from various sources. There are people who budget everything down to the last string bean and like it. They love to make lists all about Gas, Recreation,

Self-Improvement, Charity, and Taxes. (We like to make lists too, only most of ours read: Household Expenses (don't forget the pomegranate chintz for the living room chair, and four pink geraniums); Exercise Course (allow for enough lessons to take off eight pounds); Food (get that elegant olive oil from the Italian on Third Avenue)— and we make them on odd bits of paper in trains and lose them until the next time we change back to the same handbag.

Almost everyone takes a whack at good, serious budgeting now and then, however, after one of those Lessons of Life learned from being caught short because of an illness or a slump in the stock market or a love affair that called for some knock-out clothes. But if you aren't a budgeteer by nature, this probably doesn't last long. There are undoubtedly a thousand abandoned budgets for every one that is carried out to the finish. True budgeteers are born, not made, and it is our almost-immoral opinion that if you aren't one of them, you needn't shed a tear. A large number of the nicest people in the world are pretty casual about budgeting, and those who plan every peanut, stamp, and tip seem to have a Puritanical streak that must make life a little grim. We recently surrounded ourselves with books, pamphlets, and articles on the subject and even read them (more or less conscientiously), and we could scarcely keep our mind on the budgets because we were so fascinated by the number of times we came on such phrases as "mad round of gaiety," "mad pleasure seekers," "mad rush for entertainment." According to some of the charts, anyone who indulges in *anything* gayer than a semiannual trip to the movies is madly frivolous.

Our amateurish system is frankly frivolous, and why not? It does recognize, however, that you have to have some kind of a plan behind your spending if you don't want to land in debt or jail. It even has a list, made out annually and consulted infrequently. It is made out, as a matter of fact, when we are forced to decide whether we are going to renew the lease for the place in which we live. It starts with Rent, because this (or the taxes, mortgage interest, and other upkeep of your house, if you own it) ought to be the keynote of every budget plan.

Once a year, every income spender should give some serious thought to the question of how much he can spend for rent, based on the income that he feels justified in expecting. If there's a doubt in your mind as to the size of the income, take the smallest figure. This is one of the few occasions when it adds to the gaiety of life to expect the Worst. You never mind paying less than you can afford to the landlord.

Most of your expenditures will hinge around this one, whether you want them to or not, because your house is the background for living and it determines the scale on which you live, at least up to a point. Our advice is to make the amount allowed for Rent (or its equivalent) just as small as you possibly can with a smile. We are not urging a place so small that the children are underfoot most of the time and you have moments of wishing you'd never had them, nor a drab and gloomy apartment that you'll hate. We are suggesting that you make a thorough search of all the places in the locality where you plan to live that are priced slightly under what you can afford (bearing in mind the fact that a few extra blocks of walking every day probably wouldn't hurt you), and that you have an open mind as to the transforming that can be accomplished by decoration and imagination. Above all, beware of those weak moments when you think that a few dollars a month above what you can afford won't matter. A few extra dollars in rent are apt to total up to a lot of extra dollars in other things, if the place is even a little more pretentious.

Budgets worked out by our betters in this field put opposite the item of Shelter figures ranging from 20 to 30 percent of the income, and we're all for keeping it just as close to 20 percent as you can. The smaller your income, the bigger the percentage will have to be, we are sorry to say, but look a long time before you give up hope of a bargain. There is very little kick to be got out of paying the rent, and there's a lot of kick to be got out of some of the extravagances you can pay for with the money shaved off this expenditure. (But be sure that the bargain is really a bargain. A nice apartment that some friend will let you have at a discounted rate will have all the extra upkeep of the nicer apartment, and you probably can't afford it.)

The Experts don't seem to get together very well on the item of Food. We find very scientific-looking budgets, all properly balanced, putting this necessary expenditure at anywhere from 25 to 40 percent of the income, and we are surprised to discover that we do a lot better, in spite of a leaning toward artichokes and imported cheese, and with no evidence of undernourishment. Our method is to figure out, during our annual budget session, what we have been spending for meals per week, decide whether the sum can be moved up or should be cut down, and proceed accordingly. We pay cash for food and occasionally borrow from or contribute to some other item, and the system, while childish, seems to come out all right at the end of the year.

The same principle of figuring out an average weekly or monthly expenditure once a year and then following it (in a general way, but not to the last slavish penny) can be applied to all the Necessities, and we wouldn't think of listing them. There must be a thousand variations in lists of Necessities, depending on locality, size of family, standards, interests, and whether you're a Noble Character. Your list may include music lessons for Jimmie, while Miss Smith's takes in regular treatments for her arthritis. The main point in our whole theory is to shave all these unavoidables as much as you can with a clear conscience and good health.

We now come to the Great Item of the budget, which we, in our bright and original fashion, call "Miscellaneous." A lot of people get whimsical about their budgets, we notice, naming things "Oil," or "Rewards," or "Higher Life," or "G. O. K.," meaning Goodness Only Knows. (We feel a little bitter, not to say argumentative, toward the budgeteer who puts Income Tax under "Higher Life.") These fancy names are all very fine if they fool the victim, but they don't fool us long, although we admit having tried some.

135

(Account books don't seem exciting to us either, just because of the fact that they have candy-pink covers that "give you a lilt," as one writer puts it gaily, or nice bright pictures on the outside.)

"Miscellaneous" is the item that puts bubbly on the budget, and you may have guessed by now that we believe in having just as much as you can. This item, therefore, ought to be as large as you can possibly make it, by cutting down slightly on every other cut-downable item except Savings and Charity. "Miscellaneous" is the item that covers theaters and parties and trips and cocktails and permanent waves and a Wedgewood breakfast-tray set and that turquoise clip you saw in the secondhand store window and lilacs in the springtime. Only it won't cover them in most scientifically planned budgets.

We don't see the slightest necessity for dividing "Miscellaneous" up into neat little groups with appropriate headings and keeping each type of expenditure within the listed amount. (And we don't believe the expert who writes, "Later on, when you are interested in budget data, you will subdivide food into milk and cheese, which should take one-fifth of the food money." It'll certainly be a lot later on with us!) The fact is that when we've tried the more elaborate system, it hasn't worked. Our days don't work out that way, and we get all mixed up and into a dither. It's a lot simpler just to draw what we can afford for "Miscellaneous" out of the bank once a week (or half of it twice a week, so that we'll have less cash around to get lost) and do as many of the things we want to do as we can, keeping in mind the number of days the money has to cover.

This system may be slightly moronic, but it saves a lot of wear and tear and irritation. We don't know why everybody has to be a trained accountant anyway. The idea is to live within your means, and if you do it comfortably and without too much worry, the method and records seem unimportant.

But there's nothing unimportant about "Miscellaneous," and it's our inexpert but unshakable conviction that it's a badly neglected item, and it's time somebody paid it a little more ardent attention. Not only do the professional budgeteers minimize it, in the majority of cases, but most of the amateurs put down opposite this head whatever happens to be left over when they've worked out the rest of their budget (or copied it out of a book), and it's seldom if ever enough. It's true that if your income is small, this item has to be very small, there being a limit to the skimping you can do on such things as rent, food, and wardrobe, but with every increase in income, you can give

"Miscellaneous" a good deal more than its proportionate share. It's the fun and the flavor and the trimming in your life, and these are things that shouldn't be overlooked.

Our one word of warning is that a lot of things people think are bubbly don't give their money's worth. You can slip into minor extravagances that become so automatic that they give you scarcely any fun at all—like having a newspaper delivered to your door and buying another on the subway every day. You don't read either through, and what you'd save in a year by not buying the extra one would pay for a chic new evening purse or a really good bottle of brandy.

We said a few pages back that budgeting was pretty personal and, at the risk of being repetitious, may we urge you not to follow the budget worked out by Miss Mary Brown or Mrs. John Wintergreen, even though the first is the head of the woman's department in the largest bank in town and the second has been teaching economics in the high school for fifteen years and both know much more about financial matters than you do? Neither knows one quarter as much about your tastes and your life as you do, and these should be the basis of your budget. It's a good idea, to be sure, to study a couple of classic budgets before you start on your own. As with etiquette, you'd better know What's What before going in for variations. But once you do know, don't worry about the other person's rules. Make your own rules.

Our own unorthodox plan gives "Miscellaneous" slightly more than 30 percent of our income and we don't begrudge it a nickel. What's more, the fact that we haven't come on a printed budget to justify us hasn't cost us a moment's sleep.

The more conventional budgeteers will urge you to make the item of Savings as large as possible, and here we can join the chorus. Not so much because it's sensible, however, as because we have observed that most people seem to get as much fun out of buying a bond as out of buying a bracelet, once they've tried it. Owning a bond may not give you the feeling of security that it once did, but it gives you a fine feeling of importance. That money-in-the-bank strut appears to be very satisfying, and it's nice to observe that it's no longer a purely masculine goose step.

All in all, we're afraid it's wise to budget, one way or another. It seems to be the only sure method of knowing even approximately how you're coming out financially on the inevitable days of reckoning. And not knowing how you're going to manage to pay the grocer can spoil even the taste of champagne. If it doesn't, it ought to.

To come back to our theme song (about which we admit being pretty relentless) be *very* sure that your budget covers the bubbly and the orchids. The whole point of budgeting is that it simplifies life—and life, if it's worth having—is more than drudgery and bookkeeping and practicalities. Have a budget, and follow it, but don't have too severe and sternly sensible a budget. If you do, it'll ride you. You ought to ride the budget.

CASES

Case XXVI: Miss C.—Miss C. is a young lady who, when confronted with a choice between Silk and Milk, instinctively takes Silk. Unfortunately, she had to make this choice almost constantly when she first came from the Deep South to make her way in the world in Chicago.

Miss C. has blond curls, a winning way, and an appealing Southern accent, and she got a job soon after reaching the big city, but her salary wasn't much to boast about. She was paid every Saturday morning, and on her way back to the room that she had taken, she had to pass several blocks of shop windows full of such temptations as near-coral jewelry, satin pajamas, and ruffled organdy evening gowns. Miss C. never seemed to get home with more than a fraction of her meager wages, but she just couldn't see why she had so much trouble in paying the rent and practically always had to get along with one meal on Fridays. This, she felt, was very strange indeed, because the room didn't cost quite a third of her salary and she didn't eat much on the other days either.

A friend at the office suggested that Miss C. should make out a budget and offered to help her, but Miss C. thought it was pretty silly to think that money would go further just because you wrote down what you spent in a little book. Besides, it was bad enough to have your money disappear without being reminded of it all the time.

She had arrived in Chicago in the late summer, bringing a coat of light weight that was warm enough the year round at home, and long before winter came, she had used up the small capital that might have bought her a winter coat. In the autumn, her practical office mate urged her to put aside a small weekly sum, and as the days grew chillier, even Miss C. began to think this might be a good idea and decided to start next week. But somehow winter arrived before Miss C.'s next week, and a day came when she had to decide between staying at home (and probably losing her job in the end) and getting pneumonia.

Miss C. got pneumonia, and this would be a very sad story indeed if her ingenuous blond curls and Southern accent hadn't moved the heart of one young doctor in the hospital. Fortunately, he knew how to make budgets and, just before the wedding, he worked out a brand-new one with Miss C. as one of the largest items.

Case XXVII: Mr. M.—Mr. M. is a passionate budgeteer. He was born thrifty and only a kind heart kept him from being stingy. All his life he has loved keeping neat little books, which were not so little as the seasons galloped by. His favorite item has always been Savings, and no emergency (not even matrimony) ever kept him from being able to write the full quota down every month opposite this admirable head.

Mr. M.'s carefully tended savings, lovingly invested in stocks and bonds, grew and multiplied under his watchful eyes. His beautiful budgets worked like a doctor's prescription, and Life was as it should be.

It was as it should be, that is, till along about 1929, when something seemed to happen to Mr. M.'s system. It became increasingly difficult to make the figures in his neat account books correspond with those on his beloved budgets. Savings, in particular—the best-loved item of all—began to shrink. Not even the frantic attention paid it by Mr. M. stopped the steady decline. By 1933, the monthly figure opposite Savings was very close to zero, and Mr. M. had lost twenty pounds.

"What does it matter?" Mrs. M. enquired mildly from time to time. "We still live comfortably and about as we always did, and we have everything we need. What difference does it make if our savings *never* get any bigger? What are savings for anyway, if not for emergencies like this?"

This heretical question, Mr. M. felt, only showed more than ever that women didn't understand about business. His budgets had always proved his ability. Now they didn't seem to prove anything.

Mr. M.'s weight and his budgets were both getting into a really serious state when the upturn came. They are back to normal now, but Mr. M. will never again feel that Life is quite as it should be.

Case XXVIII: Miss K.—Miss K. quite frankly hasn't a head for figures. She doesn't like to keep accounts, and they don't balance when she does keep them, and budgets seem to her to be as complicated as the most difficult crossword puzzle.

But Miss K., in spite of this quality, is a bright young woman and she has to live on what she makes. And she has discovered from sad experience that you must have an outline of what you can spend if you don't want to run into serious financial difficulties. She has therefore worked out a Secret System, which she follows scrupulously but wouldn't tell anyone but her most intimate friends on a bet. It consists merely in owning six small flat silk purses, each in a different color and all bought at a discount store. When her salary is paid her, she puts a certain proportion in each purse, and pays for things accordingly. Black is for Rent, white is for Savings, red is for Clothes, and green, blue, and brown cover her other requirements. Miss K. borrows brazenly from the various purses, putting her I O U's in place of the money and usually paying back.

About a year ago, the white silk purse got so full that Miss K. had to use an old handbag, but last month, she put the contents into the savings bank and went back to the white silk purse. She calls her system Budgeting for Backward, but, as she says herself, at least she knows where she stands and doesn't find the knowledge too painful.

Case XXIX: Miss B.—Miss B. is an optimistic young woman who makes budgets religiously but can find any number of excuses for straying from them. Usually, she doesn't stray far, but recently a new temptation appeared in the not-unusual shape of a young man.

He was a beautiful young man, and Miss B. bent all her energies to snaring him into captivity. She bought clothes with a lavishness that bore no relation to the figures on her current budget. She trailed beside him in chiffon, fluttered beside him in organdy, and strode beside him in tweeds, none of which she could afford, and she served him wines of a superlative quality that he didn't recognize.

Unfortunately, he did recognize that Miss B. was out of his reach, since he was an ambitious young man, just getting a business start and living on a small salary. When his vacation came around, he went back home and married the girl who had always lived across the street and who thought cocktails were something you served at *very* special parties.

CHAPTER NINE

NINE OLD LADIES

ONE OF the fallacies of youth is that you think you won't find economizing a problem when you're older and not getting around much anyway. All of our observation makes us pretty certain that, while the average older woman may not get around so much, she likes to have things get to her—comfort and service and just as much luxury and elegance and pleasure as are possible. The ones who manage this the best have the best time. Being a Grand Old Lady, or a Picturesque one, or a Charming one, may not be as gay as being a popular debutante, but it's not to be sniffed at. It's a lot better than just letting old age overtake you and do with you as it pleases, turning you into a lonely and not-too-sweet-tempered person.

Even with financial limitations, there are plenty of ways of making life very pleasant indeed (given reasonably good health), in spite of the handicaps brought with the years. One of the chief requisites seems to be to recognize the fact that life is a circle around you, tiny when you're a child, wider and wider—as wide, in fact, as you make it—as you grow older, and narrowing again when you're frankly old. You can keep it from shrinking for a long time, perhaps, but there comes a day when it's better to look on it as a small but enchanted circle and make it as pleasant a spot as you can.

Just how pleasant this can be doesn't seem to depend on how much you can afford either. It still depends on technique. All the rules hold good to the last gasp. We base this theory on the nine old ladies whose stories make up this chapter.

CASES

Case XXX: Mrs. E.—The fact that Mrs. E. is well over seventy and has two daughters and three sons, all married and prosperous, does not seem to her to be a reason for sitting back and disintegrating. In recent years, she has had very little income, and all of her children have urged her to come to live with them. They would *love* to have her, they say, but Mrs. E. knows better. Besides, if she did move in with one of them, she is sure that she would soon be expected to stay home with the grandchildren in the evening. They get along very nicely now with the servants, and Mrs. E. doesn't see why she should give up her bridge club.

Mrs. E. therefore has for some years been House Mother in a working-girls' club in which she was very much interested in her more affluent days when her husband was living. She has an attractive room, with her own furniture and a comfortable bath. The meals are excellent, and there is enough going on to keep her busy without going out often—which would be an effort at her age. Her friends come to tea with her, and the girls in the club are fond of her and tell her most of their problems, often asking her advice and occasionally even taking it. And the many contacts of her past life and her children's present life enable her to bring a variety of interesting people to the club for lectures and entertainment, and without expense.

Mrs. E's. persistent independence keeps her children in a state of devotion tinged with a feeling of guilt, which is unreasonable but good for them. The two who live in the city come to see her frequently, send their cars for her when she goes to see them, and shower her with flowers and calf's-foot jelly (which she detests) when she has a cold. The others send her presents and occasionally drag her off on a short trip during which they lavish every possible luxury on her. They also make generous contributions to the club, which would insure Mrs. E.'s staying on, even if she wasn't such a success on her own.

Mrs. E. thoroughly enjoys life and intends to go on being House Mother right up to her final illness.

Case XXXI: Mrs. Y.—All her life, Mrs. Y. has had a sense of the dramatic. Before she was twenty-five, she was a belle, deliberately and with a success that made her famous in the community. For the next forty years, she was an adored wife, a role that she played charmingly, and when her husband died, leaving little money behind him, and it was obviously necessary for her to play still a third part, she decided to go in for being a Sweet Old Lady.

It was no longer possible for her to live in the city on her very limited means, so she found herself a small cottagey house in a New England town on the coast, where she had spent many summers and had many friends. The rent was absurdly small and the place was a perfect background for the life she planned to lead. She proceeded to go in for antiques (chiefly from her old townhouse), an old-fashioned garden, and a general effect of picture-calendar sweetness. This proved an interest which she thoroughly enjoyed, and while many of the most successful details of the picture she created were as unfamiliar to Mrs. Y. (who had been as chic and sophisticated as the next in her time) as though she had taken up Korean customs, that little fact didn't stop her. The role, she figured, was the most flattering to her age of any she could afford, and very comfortable besides.

Mrs. Y. had always been pretty and she was no less so now that she was plump and white haired instead of slim and dark. She made no effort to minimize these changes in her appearance. Instead, she sent for catalogs from all the best stores and bought flower-sprigged muslins and soft challis that she had made into fichu-ed dresses that made her look like a miniature. She also ordered patterned calicos and dimities to make into crisp window curtains, and had her maid-of-all-work practise up on old-fashioned menus that included crullers, apple pie, and even peppermint tea.

Once her background was fairly well perfected, Mrs. Y. began inviting friends and relations to visit her. The restful charm of the town, the accessibility of the ocean, and Mrs Y. herself with her picturesque background combined to make the invitations extremely popular. Some of the recipients made short visits as guests, others made longer ones as paying guests. All of them were so anxious to come again that Mrs. Y. has enough invitations in return to enable her to spend six weeks of the worst winter weather each year away from home at no expense.

Case XXXII: Miss. G. and Mrs. W.—Miss G. and Mrs. W., who are numbers three and four of these nine old ladies, were girlhood friends and lived near each other in a small Midwestern city after they grew up, continuing their close friendship. Mrs. W. married very well and had a nice house, a maid, and a hired man who drove the car when he wasn't working in the garden and around the house. Miss G.'s father left her a small income, which wouldn't have gone far in a larger place but enabled her to live comfortably in the old homestead in her hometown.

Then the Depression came, carrying off Mr. W., who had always been a worrier, cutting down the amount of money Mrs. W. could spend, and halving poor Miss G.'s small income. Both ladies were far from young, and everything seemed to be in a pretty bad way.

"Still," said some of the inevitable friends who are so good at fixing things for other people, "they can live together, and Mrs. W. can give up the car, and they ought to be able to get along all right."

But Mrs. W. didn't want to give up the car, which she liked riding in better than any other pastime. And neither of them wanted to live together. Miss G. liked being surrounded by her own possessions, and she always had her breakfast at seven-thirty and didn't intend to change. Mrs. W. liked breakfast when she woke up, which was generally much later than seven-thirty. At their age, such points are important.

Mrs. W. stayed right on in her house, letting her maid go and keeping her hired man for a few hours a day—an arrangement that meets with severe disapproval from all of her friends. Someday, they say, she will die in her bed all alone in that house. The probability doesn't alarm Mrs. W., who feels that she has to die sometime, preferably in her bed, alone or not.

Miss G. has rented two inexpensive rooms in the house just opposite Mrs. W. and brought her favorite possessions with her. She gets her breakfasts in her room and she and Mrs. W. get and eat dinner together, sharing the expense, in Mrs. W.'s kitchen and dining room.

The triumphant detail of their lives is that they still have the car and every day they go for a ride. The somewhat stately conveyance is now old enough to cause a few smiles as it rolls majestically along the countryside under the hired man's guidance. Mrs. W. and Miss G., however, prefer its comfort to the current low-seated models and, they point out, it still gets them where they want to go. Frequently, they plan a trip to another town or, in the summer, to some spot where the scenery is particularly lovely. They usually invite guests, and the guests often take them to lunch at some inn or bring a well-stocked tea basket along.

Mrs. W. and Miss G. have become authorities on the historical data in their part of the state and plan to write a book about it next winter when the weather gets too bad for them to take long drives. They are more devoted friends than ever, but extremely grateful that they don't have to live together.

Case XXXIII: Mrs. de M.—Mrs. de M. is a widow with a daughter who is married to a pleasant, but impecunious young man. While Mrs. de M. likes her son-in-law well enough, she has little if any confidence in his ability to make a fortune. She herself has an income that is far from large, but considerably larger than theirs, and her particular problem has been how to help them without seeming to do so.

After her daughter's marriage, Mrs. de M.'s friends urged her to live with the children, but Mrs. de M. was wiser than that. She thought the matter over carefully and finally decided to put a considerable proportion of her worldly goods in a small "mother-in-law" house. This house has a main section with five rooms, and a wing that contains, on the first floor, a large living room with a dining alcove and kitchenette. Upstairs, it has a bedroom and bath, with a day bed (for a possible guest) in the bedroom alcove. Each floor connects with the main part of the house by a door that is usually kept closed.

The understanding is that Mrs de M.'s daughter and her husband live in the main part of the house so that Mrs. de M. won't be alone and unprotected. (Nothing is said of the fact that they couldn't possibly live so comfortably otherwise.) Mrs. de M., of course, lives in the wing, and she insists on Living Her Own Life. She gets most of her own meals, entertains her own guests for tea or bridge or dinner, and goes as she pleases to club and church meetings. She never goes into the main part of the house when her son-in-law is home except on invitation or after telephoning that she is coming, and it is comparatively seldom that she goes without warning even when he isn't, since she is wise enough to know that a continuous popping in and out would completely take away that feeling of privacy to which every grown-up is entitled.

Needless to say, her attitude triples the devotion of the children. They constantly invite her for meals, the daughter consults her on a hundred subjects (on which she would probably resent unsolicited advice, just as you would), and she almost always urges her to come along too on any shopping expedition.

Mrs. de M. has figured out that, at her death, her daughter can use the entire house, if the son-in-law proves to be more successful than she expects; if not, the wing can be rented to some Extra Woman or young couple and bring in a small income.

Case XXXIV: Mrs. S.—Mrs. S. (sixth of these nine old ladies) is in a financial situation that corresponds almost exactly with Mrs. de M.'s, but the resemblance stops right there. Mrs. S. is a domineering old lady, and the fact that her two children (both of whom are married) are not very well off and that even a part of her small income can help them, seems to her ample justification for running them and her grandchildren as completely as possible. (We suspect that she would find some other justification if she didn't have this one.) She lives with her daughter's family six months of the year and with her son's the other six months, paying her board and getting her money's worth with interest.

Either family would be delighted to scrape along somehow without Mrs. S.'s assistance (and so much of her company), but Mrs. S. won't hear of it. She agrees when they suggest tactfully that she could afford to live in a nice boardinghouse and that she'd be much more comfortable, but she says she wouldn't think of leaving them like that. She's shared and sacrificed for her family all her life, and she isn't going to stop now. Neither, if the truth were told, is she going to stop putting her finger into each and every pie undertaken by her descendants. Her daughter's social life (what little she can manage to have), her daughter-in-law's housekeeping, her son's job, and her son-in-law's personal habits, not to mention the studies, manners, pastimes, and beaux of her grandchildren—Mrs. S. can and does tell how to fix them all.

Her children have every desire to give her all the devotion that's due her, but they sometimes wish it didn't have to be Mother's Day three hundred and sixty-five days in the year.

Case XXXV: Miss R.—Miss R., at a somewhat advanced age, inherited a large, old-fashioned house, but not the wherewithal to live in it. This, however, did not discourage Miss R. She liked the house, and she liked the neighborhood, and she felt that having to bestir herself in order to live there would merely keep her young and interested. She therefore engaged a struggling, not-too-high-priced young architect to make some plans for remodeling it into several apartments at the least possible expense, bearing in mind the fact that she planned to rent only to women who were more or less her contemporaries and who would prefer old-fashioned atmosphere to new-fangled decoration.

This part of the plan proved to be the secret of Miss R.'s success. In the first place, it reduced the cost of the alterations, and it kept them within Miss R.'s taste and understanding. It also developed a house that attracted exactly those she wanted to attract—women of similar tastes and interests who provided companionship as well as cash. (Miss R. is one of the rare older women who recognize not merely that different generations look at practically everything differently, but also that there's no reason why they shouldn't.)

When the plans were submitted, it looked as though they would use up a pretty large proportion of Miss R.'s meager capital, but again she refused to give up. Instead, she discussed them with any and all of her friends, arousing so much interest that she had her boarders lined up in advance and a small income assured. The final decorations were done to suit each tenant, who could scarcely wait to move in and who has had no wish to move out again. For while each one has her own home and does as she pleases, together they can make up a bridge table without going out in bad weather, or hold a reading club at a moment's notice. More important still, nobody feels timid with the others so close by.

Recently, the eldest of Miss R.'s tenants died, and before the funeral, four older women telephoned to ask if they might rent the vacant apartment.

Case XXXVI: The Misses T.—The Misses T. have lived for years in a comfortable square brick house in a medium-size city, and when, a few years ago, their income began

to shrink, they felt that they were too old to pull up roots and move. Besides, they were both hale and hearty, and they had been equal to all the emergencies to date and didn't see why they couldn't meet any new ones. They not only knew everybody in town, but they'd known most people's mothers too, a circumstance that they felt ought to be a distinct advantage.

Miss Sarah T., who is pink-and-white and plump, had long been famous for her cooking and she opened a cooking school for the engaged girls of the city two mornings a week in the sunny kitchen overlooking the garden at the back of the house. A surprising number of pupils flock to her classes, egged on by Love and fond mamas, and Miss Sarah is confident that her training in biscuit making and the cooking of a good roast is going to cut down the number of future divorces in that vicinity. Miss Jane, who is angular and more executive, rents the two living rooms to various women's clubs or for bridge parties in the afternoon, serving tea, sandwiches, and little cakes, which the sisters make on the mornings when the kitchen has no classes. She often has the rooms engaged for four or more afternoons a week, which makes it possible for them to keep old Katie to do all the cleaning and also gives the Misses T. a chance to see their old friends and acquaintances, and know more about the goings-on of the city than the Society Editors of the local papers.

CHAPTER TEN

WHEN YOU'RE REALLY BROKE

HAVING SAID that too stringent economy was out of this book, we are now going to break down and say a few words on that very subject. We're not pretending that it's a gay one or that we're going to be very cheery about it. For what we really mean is something more than stringent economy; we mean not knowing where your next meals— or at any rate, your meals next month—are coming from, which is a predicament you can't laugh off. And we'd like to state right now that if you don't like sermons, you'd better turn back to Chapter Six, which is all about food.

The sensation of having little or nothing in your pocket, no job, and no backlog to turn to is like crossing a raging river on a plank without a railing, only a lot more frightening. And there is the additional element of hurt pride, which hurts more than most physical ailments and for which anaesthetics are not supplied. Most people, and especially most men, would rather admit ignorance, dissipation, being jilted, and a collection of physical disabilities than having no bank account. They'd rather experience them too, simultaneously if necessary. Having a mind above material things is all very well in books, but in real life there aren't many Gandhis.

No words of ours will make a dent in the fact that every day you spend without enough money to pay for actual necessities will be a special form of Purgatory, and that, the world being as it is, this is probably as it should be. There is something definitely wrong with people who don't mind needing to be helped. It may happen to the best of us, but that doesn't mean that we should like it. When you stop minding, when being helped becomes a habit, you're on the skids, and if you don't do something about it pretty quickly, it's going to be too late.

One of the first danger signals is the well-known feeling that the world owes you a living. It doesn't; you owe it something worth paying for. When you don't come across, there's usually trouble ahead. When the trouble is financial, most people find it painful, and it usually leaves a mark.

It may, however, be a good mark and valuable later on—though you won't think so until considerably later on.

Hurt pride, in this particular emergency, is something you've got to stand, but not to the extent that most people do. For the average person feels that the moment his purse is empty he'll be considered a failure and looked at with suspicion besides.

He's right, insofar as strangers and most casual acquaintances are concerned (including you, if you don't know him well), but not in respect to his friends. And, as a matter of fact, at this particular stage of our national history, even some of the strangers will think not, as he supposes, "That fellow can't be much good," but—with a shiver up their spines—"If he's in this fix now, maybe I'll be there tomorrow."

There are comparatively few of us, these uncertain days, who, even if we haven't been in this unfortunate situation, haven't caught a glimpse of it looming on the horizon, and near enough to be recognizable too. And most of the exceptions have done a little worrying about someone who has met it face-to-face and whom they've wanted to help and couldn't.

One spar to catch at is the fact that people do want to help. The right people, at any rate. Cynics who don't believe this just aren't very observant—if they were, they'd see that practically everybody is made uncomfortable by seeing other people suffer and will do almost anything to avoid being uncomfortable. Moreover, helping you is a move against the day when they themselves may need a helping hand. But more than any of this, the average normal person is genuinely kind.

But no one can help you if you don't give him a chance. If you're really broke, the quickest and least painful thing for you to do is to tell your story to a friend. You'll hate it (and so will he), but you've got yourself into a place where you'll hate anything you do anyway.

We really mean got yourself into it. For it is our cold-blooded opinion that this situation is seldom altogether a matter of hard luck. A good many willing workers and capable people have a series of bad breaks, but they have usually put a little something by for just such emergencies, or they have made connections or a reputation that helps them to another job before the crisis is too acute, and far more often, it's not bad breaks that are back of being broke. Even the poor starving widow with several small children has frequently, if the truth were known, passed up a few opportunities to build up a small savings account or made it difficult for her husband to save up for investments. There is a lot more justice than most of us will admit, even to ourselves. And most of the saddest hard luck stories can be explained by the victim's character, once you know him well enough.

To go back to the question of friends—perhaps you haven't any close enough to justify your going to him for help. Then you'll have to tell your story to somebody else, which won't be so easy, but before we go into that—why haven't you any such friend? This is something you'd better stop and think about right now, for the answer is probably one reason why you're in the dilemma.

Everybody ought to have friends. Any grown-up who hasn't deserves a little suspicion. Unless you live on a desert island or a lighthouse off some high and rocky coast, you are in pretty constant contact with people, and there's something wrong if an occasional bond doesn't spring up between you and a few of them. A real bond that will stand a slight strain—like lending you money or helping you get a job.

Friends are not just social assets. Getting on with people, and getting close to some of them, is an important part of living. It's part of getting and holding a job, as well as having fun. If you're not at least reasonably good at it, it's time you did some serious self-investigating.

There are plenty of people who don't hold with this theory. As likely as not, they will be a little superior when they tell you that they are born hermits or that they don't stoop to being tolerant and friendly. These are people with a blind spot.

To get back to the friend you do have, let him help you, but not too much or too often. If he thinks it's too much or too often before you do, this is another thing you'd better do something about. You are justified in turning to the friend in an emergency, just as you are justified in getting help when you are sick, but you've got to carry on from there, and a very good thing too. If you aren't willing and anxious to do that much, there's not much hope for you anyway.

You *can* carry on from there. And this is something to remember from the first hour of catastrophe. It's the people who feel certain that the emergency is temporary, a circumstance that might happen to anybody, and never let anything shake their belief, who are out of the woods the quickest. Such people have courage and faith in themselves, and you can't keep them down. They don't cringe or get an inferiority complex, even though they're to blame for the whole situation and know it. They know, too, that everybody makes mistakes, and a lot of people have been in just the same place and got themselves out of it. The ones who tell you you won't get a second chance are usually the ones who haven't spunk enough to make a second chance. There are dozens of chances for the people who go out and get them, but not always one for those who wait for the chance to come.

The fact that you aren't quite as young as you used to be doesn't let you out either. The old-fashioned notion that flaming youth gets the jobs and eventually the cash, is slipping. Look around at the people you know and you'll probably find that a pretty big proportion had their success in middle life and some of them in lines that they took up after forty.

There is a job ready for most people who are willing to work and aren't too high hat about the kind of work they will do. We mean really work, however. It may take persistency and ingenuity to find the job, but it's probably there, though you may not be ready for the job. Most people haven't developed a quarter of the ability they should have, and you may need quite a lot of preparation to fit you for the kind of job you'll like. But even if your school days are a long way behind you, that needn't stop you. It won't, if you've got what it takes.

There are a number of things that you can do, and one of them (we warned you that this was going to be a sermon) is to go to church. Church is an excellent place to think, though thinking is something that takes practice, and you may have to go to a good many services before you get into the swing of it. Clear and honest thinking is one form of worship (and not the lowest form either), and no one who does it sufficiently is permanently out of a job. But this doesn't mean going to church and waiting, however patiently, for the service to be over. Worship is an active and not a passive process, though the activity may consist in slipping into a back pew in an empty church and sitting there. But not in sitting there in a coma, waiting for a light to descend upon you. You've got to make a definite mental effort, and it may take some time to see results, but they are usually worth waiting for.

You may wonder what all this has to do with bubbly on your budget. Nothing at all, actually. This chapter is about a possible (though we hope not a probable) period when you haven't a budget and aren't entitled to bubbly. And don't forget that you aren't entitled to the bubbly.

Being really broke may be a desperate experience, and we're a lot more sympathetic about it than we sound. But it's most desperate when you begin to be resentful of the people who aren't broke; when you begin to spend other people's money and think that Mrs. Smith might buy you the coat you wanted and Mr. Jones might lend you his automobile. That is the time when being broke has you down.

If, on the other hand, Mrs. Smith's coat merely causes you to make a mental note that you'll buy one like that for yourself a couple of years from now; if you can still forget your troubles at a party and not make everyone else remember them; if you never lose your determination to make good, given time—then being broke will be a profitable, though not a pleasant experience. You will have learned that having life by the tail is not a matter of dollars and cents; it's a feeling of power that can master an emergency. Once you have that, you have Something.

CASES

Case XXXVII: Mrs. T.—Some years ago, Mrs. T. (who was then Miss F.) gave up a position that enabled her to live comfortably in New York, in order to live uncomfortably with Mr. T. in a variety of places. Mr. T. is a writer who has charm, ability, and wanderlust, but who, when (as happens semioccasionally) he has enough money to enable them to settle down, immediately spends it for tickets to some yet unvisited country.

Since her marriage, Mrs T. has almost starved in Budapest, Shanghai, Madrid, Moscow, and on the Left Bank. She has learned to bargain with pennies in half a dozen languages, to cajole irate landlords into friendliness, to make strange garrets homelike, and to get along on sketchy and irregular meals. She has half forgotten the meaning of the word *security*, and she never lets herself love a possession too dearly, knowing that she will have to give it up sooner or later.

She has also learned that, given wits and courage, you don't starve. And if you should catch her in an intimate moment, you would find that she knows, too, that an affection that will last through the crises she and her husband have experienced is more compensating than money, and that color and adventure in life are not dependent on your pocketbook.

Mrs. T. still hopes that someday they will settle down and live like other people, but she knows that if they don't, she will live happily anyway and—even more important—very little that can happen now will frighten her. She realizes that that very fact is a possession worth more, perhaps, than all she's given up, or any other gift that Mr. T. could buy her.

Case XXXVIII: Mrs. O.—Mrs O. is an orchidaceous lady who enjoyed every luxury until she was forced to divorce Mr O., and even that unfortunate episode didn't stop her altogether. Instead, she put all her energy and ingenuity into business and, with surprising rapidity, built up a small advertising firm that catered to expensive manufacturers and enabled her to go on buying Schiaparelli gowns, Lelong perfume, and white roses for her living room.

Eventually, however, the Depression came and Mrs. O.'s fancy clients were among the first casualties. One by one, they fell by the wayside, leaving Mrs. O. with no business and, finally, with no bank account. So acute was the emergency that she was forced to give up not merely her office, but also her apartment, and to borrow money from one relative and go to live with another.

We now come to the miracle personified by Mrs. O. For today, some time after the crisis, she is still friends with both relatives.

During the year and a half when things were getting no better, she continued to be a reluctant guest, and, what's more, she did it with such amiability that no one else was conscious of the reluctance. Not that she didn't hate it as much as you would, but Mrs. O. is a philosophical lady who realizes that there's no use making a fuss about things while they can't be helped.

The backbone of Mrs. O.'s remarkable fortitude (and we can think of few situations requiring more fortitude) was her belief that the situation was temporary and her never-failing hope that it would be over next week. So firm was her conviction that it spread to her hostess, who—instead of feeling imposed on (as she would certainly have felt had she known the visit was going to last a year and a half)—was kept in a constant dither lest her guest fly away at any moment. This we regard as a high pinnacle of triumph.

Never during her enforced stay did Mrs. O. apologize too profusely or grow humbly grateful, though she was punctilious in expressing her gratitude briefly and sincerely on occasion. When she was able to leave, both her hostess and the upstairs maid shed several tears, but we are forced to admit that Mrs. O. could scarcely wait to get into her new one-room apartment.

Mrs. O.'s business is still not quite what it used to be, but her recent training enables her to live on almost the old scale on her new and much smaller income. She even—very occasionally—has squab at her dinners and orchids in her Lalique bowl. But she has paid back both relatives—one in cash and one in loyalty and devotion.

Case XXXIX: Mrs. U.—For fifteen years Mrs. U. was the wife of an Old-School Husband who didn't believe that she should have to bother her pretty head with masculine matters like money and who doled out a little cash (a very little) when he felt like it and gave her charge accounts at half a dozen shops. The fact that Mrs. U. felt humiliated by this arrangement and by never having any money in her pocketbook didn't seem important to Mr. U. He could tend to the financial matters in the family, he said, and he continued his chivalrous system (which has prevented so many dissatisfied wives from going to Reno) until, for a number of reasons, Mrs. U. decided, one bright spring morning, that she couldn't stand Mr. U. any longer.

This decision was complicated by the fact that Mrs. U.'s sheltered life had kept her in complete ignorance of most practical affairs. It almost looked as if Mrs. U. would have to choose between starvation and Mr. U. After some consideration, she decided to try starvation.

During the first month after leaving Mr. U., with her personal belongings packed in two large Vuitton bags and a handsome dressing case, it looked as though Mrs. U. might really starve. Not wishing to meet her friends, who were also Mr. U.'s friends, she sold the dressing-case, one bag, and about half of her clothes and lived at a girls' club in a remote and far from smart section of the city, while she walked miles every day in search of work. Although she didn't enjoy the period, she knew, even while she was going through it, that it was teaching her several things. First, that even new friends who had little more than she had were ready to share with her when it was a matter of necessity—a reassuring discovery. Second, that no one should have been allowed to reach her age without knowing how to do *something*. And third, that she really did prefer her present, often-hungry situation to the one arranged by Mr. U.

When she finally got work in a small shop, she fell to with such enthusiasm that she did well from the first. This, combined with taste and knowledge of clothes, set her on the path to a small but exciting success. She gets a thrill out of every kitchen pan or bit of maple furniture that she can buy for her very small establishment— and even more of a thrill out of the fact that—if she ever should meet Mr. U. again—she can tell him exactly what she thinks of him.

Case XL: Miss Q.—Miss Q. is one of the thousands of people in the world who have met with reverses, but she is unconscious of the other thousands. Fate has taken a special crack at her, she feels, and she can't understand why all her acquaintances don't pour sympathy (and gifts) over her poor head. Here she is, left suddenly with next to no income and with no hope ahead, all through no fault of her own. She isn't strong either (few people are if they sit and mope as much as Miss Q.). And she seldom goes anywhere, because she hasn't a car, and the neighbors, she says, are selfish with theirs. (She has never noticed that the neighbors have all they can do to make their cars serve their whole families and their friends, and still get time out for repairs.) And she *never* has anything new because she can't afford to buy things, and her aunts aren't very generous. It's a hard world.

Maybe it is, but it would be a lot harder if it were full of people like Miss Q. If she would go out and do a little work, she could buy herself a few of the things she mourns for—and we wouldn't be surprised if people would even make room for her in their cars. (But we wouldn't count on this, Miss Q. It's better to walk than to sponge.)

MARJORIE HILLIS (1889–1971) worked for *Vogue* for more than twenty years, beginning as a captions writer for the pattern book and working her way up to assistant editor of the magazine itself. In 1936 she wrote *Live Alone and Like It,* the superlative guide for "bachelor ladies." It was an instant best-seller and was followed by this book, originally titled *Orchids on Your Budget.*